The Work Trap

The Work Trap:
Solving the Riddle of Work and Leisure

by
Martin C. Helldorfer

Affirmation Books
Whitinsville
Massachusetts

With gratitude I express my indebtedness to Drs. Bert van Croonenburg, Douglas Steere, James Leahy, Charles Reutemann, William Batt, and Paul Hebert for their inspiration as well as assistance.

I voice my special indebtedness to Marie Colette Hanlon of the Sisters of Charity. Without her I could not have written, nor would I have desired to write, this essay.

M. C. H.

Skaneateles, New York

Published with ecclesiastical permission
Second edition
Copyright 1981, 1983 by House of Affirmation, Inc.

Library of Congress Catalog Card Number: 80-52059
ISBN 0-89571-017-X (previously ISBN 0-88489-127-5)

Cover design by Rosemary Fay, S.N.D.deN.

Income derived from the sale of Affirmation books is used by the House of Affirmation in its ministry to priests and religious suffering from emotional unrest.

For Bernadette

Contents

Activity, that simple saint, cannot be bothered figuring why it rushes: enough for her devotions that there are things to do. Why should she bother? Her religion is to make by rote her rosary of perfect answers. Reflection she leaves till tomorrow. There is no need to think as candle burns and beads drop rushedly from her hand. Who dares ask why? The world she makes is all the world there is. Her faith is perfect.

—after a poem by A. MacLeish

People never just "slip" into trouble— depression, obsession, anxiety, alcoholism, perversion, chronic illness—all forms of self-destruction. They march into trouble as if by inevitable predetermination.

—K. Menninger

Introduction

This is a book about the value of human presence and the dignity of every person's work. The soil from which the reflections rise is the topics of work and leisure and the obscuring if not the total eclipse of both. If the gist of the book could be summarized by saying that many difficulties in everyday life stem from the absence of leisure, then its conclusion would be phrased in this way: we have to become involved, astoundingly more rather than less, if we wish to rediscover both work and pleasure. What is at issue is the base from which we are involved. These thoughts might seem curious. The why and how behind them form the substance of the text. I ask that you journey with me through a terrain of familiar words and possibly unfamiliar thought in an effort to recognize how wonderfully important is our presence to one another and how necessary it is to be attentive to the way in which we are present as we work, play, or pray.

It is a book written for the rich, not necessarily those with dollars, yen, or francs, but for those who have the freedom to search for significant human work. Most of the world's peoples do not have such liberty. For the poor, work is not chosen so much as it is clung to. Work, for such, when it can be found at all, is clutched with fingers that grab for life. The condition of the poor has been etched in my memory. Their presence affects my pen. I cannot avoid their stares, but I cannot write for them. What well-fed person can speak convincingly to a hungry man or woman? The eyes of the poor call for a hand, not words. I write for those among the rich who have trouble with work and leisure. We are the craftsmen, teachers, laborers, ministers, cooks, and doctors whose restless ways betray our poverty.

I publish hesitantly. The topics of work and leisure are so complex that to say anything is to be confronted with the prospect of superficiality. Yet if hesitant, I am also driven. Words, though fragile, are all that we have to touch one another. Not to voice them, no matter how hesitantly, is to reject something of the gift of being human. In face of that gift I wish to write. I ask the reader to entertain the essay as a chance guest. Ascribe my fumbling words to the nervousness of a stranger but welcome them with the same kind of trust that can slowly transform the stranger into a friend.

Martin C. Helldorfer, F.S.C.

Preface to Second Edition

The original text of *The Work Trap* is here presented without revision. Today in my workshops I find it helpful to make some useful distinctions between work-fixation, work-exhaustion, and overwork. These conditions may appear similar but differ in their origins and in the ways we can avoid them. To incorporate these distinctions into the present text would require a complete revision of the book. Because it has been helpful to many in its present form, I prefer to leave *The Work Trap* unrevised and to offer in the near future a second book expanding these new ideas.

I wish to thank Saint Mary's Press for its gracious permission to publish this second edition through the House of Affirmation. Many persons know of the ministry of the House through its six residential centers, its various educational programs, or its Affirmation books and tapes. I consider it a privilege to have this book appear as a House of Affirmation publication, and I am grateful to Rev. Dr. Thomas Kane and Sister Dr. Anna Polcino, S.C.M.M., cofounders of the House, for their support and encouragement. Finally, I want to acknowledge my indebtedness to Sister Marie Kraus, S.N.D., for her helpful editorial suggestions in republishing *The Work Trap*.

M.C.H.

June 1983   Hopedale, Massachusetts

1 Our Lives As Doers

May I tell you a story that is as true as true can be, yet fanciful in some of its details?

I was hospitalized as a young man with a pain in my lower stomach that was as severe and excruciating as any I can imagine. Doubled over as if to protect myself, I would have done anything to relieve it. If relief entailed surgery, I wanted it immediately. If nothing could be done, I wanted a drug to put me to sleep. If that meant death, I didn't care. All exercise of reason and all perspective were lost. Pain ruled. Fortunately, others had the balance that I lacked, and I did have an operation. I'm telling the story because of what happened while I was recuperating.

The first days after surgery are a blur in my memory. What I do remember is that the first person to break through my dullness was a young nurse, blond and petite. I do not know why I noticed her among all the others. Maybe it was her attractiveness; something about her voice and reserve was alluring. Perhaps it was the way that she effortlessly changed the bed linen; when sick, one cherishes every little service. Each morning I looked forward to the time when she would come to change the bed even though I lay there helplessly tied by tubes in arm, nose, and throat. Though ticklish, I grew accustomed to her hands. By rolling me from one side to the other she did the job perfectly. In no time the bed was made meticulously.

One morning (it was a memorable Wednesday) I could hear the wheels of the linen cart move down the corridor room by room. The nearer the cart came, the more alive I felt. Imagine what happened to my young heart when, instead of the nurse of my dreams, a heavy-set matronly black woman walked through the door. I do not mean to speak disparagingly of size, bearing, or race. All I am trying to say is that something of my fantasy life vanished in an instant.

The older woman changed the bed linen in exactly the same manner as the younger. She worked her hands under me in the same way and rolled me from side to side as the other had done. Yet as soon as she touched me I knew the undeniable difference between her hands and those of the more attractive younger nurse. Can hands be strong and soft at the same time? The hands of this older nurse were. What went into the making of those hands? Was she a mother? Had she suffered much? What taught her to touch as she did? Who taught her? I will never know the answers to those questions, but I have been left with the realization that we may all do the same job, we may even be technically proficient in what we do, but we do not all touch the world in the same way. What we bring to our work beyond competency and proficiency, as important as they are, is bewilderingly significant.

Few of us are nurses but all of us touch the world. The man who teaches touches others. So does the woman who writes or the person in the kitchen, office, field, or factory. We all handle the world and, even though we seldom allude to it, we bring to that activity our entire past which finds its way into our hands. How we are present as we work and how we live in moments apart from work are important. The person who knows that life is a gift handles the world in a special way. The hand warmed by compassion touches in a way that a machine cannot. We work differently after we have heard a symphony, walked in the woods, been jostled in a subway, been embarrassed by selfishness, or have rested in prayer. All of life, every moment of the past and our dreams of the future, finds its way into the present work of our hands.

We have only to look into the vacuous eyes of a broken man with few recognized talents to understand how important work is to the human spirit. Remove the opportunity for work and all talk of valuableness apart from what we do is unintelligible. Everyone craves worthwhile involvement, and all need to find it. The work need not be prestigious. Neither does it have to be what we usually term a job. What is necessary is that we are involved in a way that we know is valuable—not only to ourselves but to those about us as well.

As important as work is, it can become a problem. With little awareness and the best of intentions it is easy to slip into a work-like way of living. As that occurs we forget about life beyond the work of our hands. Reducing all of life to work, our hands can become proficient but cold. We can be involved in some of the most exciting projects and yet find ourselves questioning their importance, simply because we have forgotten our lives on the way to becoming machine-like. That is a personal tragedy for each of us but a social one as well, for we build a world in which the life of the human spirit is diminished.

How could this happen? Let us trace a pattern of possibilities using the lives of a teacher, social worker, and administrator of a housing project as examples. The first words are those of a priest.

I.

I am forty-two years old. I don't think that I have particular difficulties with sex, but I do know that something within me is changing relative to sexuality. Sometimes I think that I am going through a second adolescence. Do you know what I really want in life? I want to be close to someone. You'd think that I would have outgrown those feelings by now, wouldn't you? To say that I want intimacy in life sounds like a teenager talking, doesn't it?

I do have a few close friends. I also have plenty of people who admire me. I have almost too many of these. I don't need to be admired. I have the feeling that others feel close to me because I lead well and provide assurance for them. As incongruous as it may sound coming from a grown man, I wish that I could hold and be held. How's that statement coming from a fellow who appears so strong to others? Sometimes I dream that I will be able to lie down and rest with a loved one. Does that surprise you? Don't get me wrong. I am not talking about sex; or I don't think that I am. I am talking about closeness.

II.

You know, I'm tired. I am tired with the kind of tiredness that sleep can't cure. There is something about my life that is too heavy. I only have to think about what I have to do and I get tired. That's the truth. Sometimes the smallest things tire me. In fact I am tired most of the time. Taking a nap doesn't help. Even after rest I can't get my work done with any enthusiasm.

Some people tell me that I look as if I'm dying on my feet. I wonder about that. Yesterday someone asked me if I was sick. I chuckled, more through nervousness than from amusement. She sees something that worries me. I am tired and I know it.

III.

I am supposed to be a "religious" person. I do church work yet I flee church-people and God-talk whenever I can. There is even a way that I dislike coming here on Sundays, but I do it anyway. I know one thing for sure; if I want something interesting and enlivening to read, I certainly don't turn to religious literature. Like so much in the church, it puts me to sleep.

I don't know if it is a question of belief or not. More often than not I think that I am still a believer yet basically distrustful. Instead of the word basically, maybe I should say fundamentally. I picture most people as spontaneously trusting others. I've developed differently over the years. I envy people who can forget about themselves and seemingly enter into life with vigor. I wonder if they are not pretending.

These examples are particular to the persons involved. Their worlds may not be our world; their way of expressing themselves, not our way. Yet the examples do strike a note and give a feeling for some of the difficulties that many of us know in so many differing ways. The problem is work and what happens to us if we overwork. Not all problems nor the difficulties mentioned above are necessarily the consequences of overwork. Neither does everyone overwork. But many of us do and some of us know that we do. Also, many difficulties that we have stem from overwork. Some of us feel a kinship with the people who have expressed themselves above. Our words may differ but we know what it means to be worn down by work, to yearn to be close to others in a way that escapes us, and to be weary in a way that no amount of rest seems to relieve. We also know how it feels to grow distrustful and then detached from others to the point of wondering if anything really matters at all.

There are a host of difficulties associated with overwork that can be enumerated without need of exploration. Humor is lost and oversensitivity becomes apparent. Interests narrow; conversation apart from work is flat. We find ourselves overeating or unable to eat at all. An unbalanced diet and a lack of exercise result in health problems. As life becomes overly restricted, the stimulation we seek often takes the form of medication or addiction.

Because of our absorption in work, a distance develops between ourselves and others. Loved ones easily become strangers, and we end by isolating ourselves from others. Once that distance develops, especially if we have a strong need to justify ourselves, it is extremely difficult to change the way we live.

Accompanying these difficulties is the problem of time. Moments of relaxation become rare or nonexistent. We feel rushed and pushed. If there is something to be done we cannot rest until it is finished. When one project is over there is always another to be tackled. There is never a moment when we feel we can stop.

There is also a question of living with ourselves as well as contending with the questioning eyes of others. Why do we work so much? Why do we never seem to have time to be with others? Why do we not have time to relax or even play? We say we work incessantly because we have to . . . because we like to . . . because we are expected to . . . because we are devoted . . . because there doesn't seem to be anyone else to do it . . . because. . . . Some do work for these reasons. The difficulty is that many of us do not. The reasons that we give to explain our way of living are often attempts to justify ourselves. Other reasons are behind our activity. Which are they? What are the real reasons that we overwork? Let us leave that question for a later moment. First, let us clarify what we mean by work and then show how one can begin to live in such a way that everything becomes "work."

What meaning do the words "work," "working," and "worker" have for us? We refer to a special way of doing things and of being present. We are always doers; we are not always workers. For instance, when we play, pray, or make love, we are doing something, but we do not intend to refer to these activities as work. When we refer to work we want to accent the fact that we have a project and that this project necessitates a special kind of presence. Think of it this way. We go to the airport to meet a friend. This is a project. Suppose our friend is tall, blond, and we know that he is to arrive on a particular flight at a certain time. As we search for him we are likely to notice tall blond people coming from a specified direction at a definite time. Whom and what we perceive are determined to some extent by our project.

When we work, are working, or are workers, our chief activity is to change and shape the world about us. This is a very specialized kind of presence. Our imagination, will, sight, touch, hearing, smell, taste, and emotional life all reflect the task at hand. We become involved selectively, sensing what will help or hinder our project. We think analytically and critically. We categorize the world about us into what is useful and not-so-useful, valuable and not-so-valuable for our purposes. The world becomes a means for us to accomplish our task.

When our project is a shaping one, we have to distance ourselves from the world about us in order to move it according to our purposes. This is to hold the world apart, as it were. If we did not push it away from us a little, we would never be able to do anything. We would simply stand in admiration. Speaking with another gives us a sense of this seldom realized presence. At some point in the conversation our words may run out and the space that the project of speaking provided may disappear. As a result we are left face to face with another without a project. The closeness can even be embarrassing as eyes meet and closeness is felt.

So when we refer to ourselves as workers, we refer to a manipulative and controlling presence that is necessary and without which we cannot accomplish a task.

To think of work in this way may initially be disconcerting. Few counselors, doctors, mothers, or teachers would enjoy speaking of themselves as manipulative when working. Not many clergy would associate the word "project" with their efforts as ministers. Generally, all the words that we have used to describe the presence of the worker are considered pejorative. There is a way in which most people avoid being overly critical, highly resistive, manipulative persons. Nevertheless, we frequently have to be controlling-type persons if we wish to change the world about us. What is important is that these are not the only attitudes nor our only approach to life. The hand that controls and the eye that is critical need to be caring as well. What a difference there is between the hand of a doctor who cares and one who does not, yet both persons are analytical, critical, controlling, and selective while they work.

Often there is an embarrassment associated with recognizing the stance of the worker. None of us likes the sound of the words that differentiate the worker's stance. In our embarrassment we may be inclined to deny their truth, much like a person who is made aware of his or her selfishness. We wince, often deny, but later understand. With time we can see that we are selfish, but much more is at stake. Continued denial would practically paralyze any efforts to move away from our selfish ways.

The word "work" need not refer exclusively to one's job. It is true that a job demands work, but we often work at other times as well. Consider this example.

I know a man who cannot play with his children. He says that they make him impatient. When they sit to play a game of cards the children keep changing the rules! "How can you play if you keep changing the rules?" He does like to play tennis on Sunday mornings. "There you have definite rules and something to accomplish." I think that the fellow is a fixated worker and does not know it. The fact that he cannot play with his children is consistent with the way that he lives his life. He is a worker at everything. He tells me that he plays tennis; I suspect that he is "working" at something he enjoys.

A second example is similar in that it also illustrates the broad meaning we wish to give to the word "work."

> I also know a woman who, I believe, has reduced prayer to work without realizing it. She says that she is praying; I see her as working. She says that spontaneous prayer is the only way to pray. There is truth in the statement, but the truth for her hides a problem. She says that she cannot pray the psalms because they are not hers. I do not think that she can accept anything that is given to her, including the psalms. She always has to be a maker. Since she does not easily get into another's world, she finds it difficult to accept another person where he or she is. I see her as a worker at everything under the guise of spontaneity. She forms the world but cannot let herself be formed by it. I doubt if she has any inkling of what has happened to her.

How easy it is to approach every aspect of life in a work-like way, if this is how we understand it. But such an approach reduces our experience to a single dimension—the experience of work—even though we may give it differing names.

Sometimes we play. Other times we love. Still other times we pray. These differing activities lead us to experience life in remarkably different ways. People can get stuck in the way they experience life simply because they are always and everywhere workers. It is time to dance but they cannot or, if they do, they are so rigid and distanced that they resemble machines rather than dancers. This sometimes occurs when, for one reason or another, a person cannot change the type of presence that he or she brings to differing situations or, at other times, when a person cannot let differing situations change him or her appropriately. When it is time to play with children, such a person had better be prepared to relinquish the serious way of work. Some of us know that we cannot, and as a result we know the tediousness of having to play when we are unable. When it happens that a work-like approach to life becomes one's only approach, this special difficulty is termed *work-fixation*. Work-fixation turns every experience into work—even playing, dancing, or relaxing.

Work-fixation is not necessarily to be equated with spending long hours at an office. Nor is it necessarily avoided by spending much time pursuing leisure-time activities. Rather, work-fixation has to do with a way of living, of approaching life, and of being present to whatever we are involved in. The person who "works" from morning till night may not be at all trapped in a work-like approach to life, just as the person who has a job for a few hours each day may not necessarily avoid work-fixation. The mark of being fixated is being always and everywhere project-oriented.

Such a presence can be described in many ways. One is the way that we involve ourselves with the world of others, things, and events. To describe work-fixation in this manner is to speak of seeing the world as something to be used, of experiencing ourselves as driven, and of living in such a way as to control and protect what we are always and everywhere constructing.

A second way to describe work-fixation is in terms of space and time. This approach speaks of a sense of time urgency on the one hand and a sense of being either too close to or too distanced from life on the other.

We will come back to both ways of speaking about work-fixation. For the moment, however, and despite the danger, let us speak of it in terms of behavior. We are going to interpret behavior from the outside, as it were, disregarding a host of considerations apart from the behavior itself. This is always dangerous but the risk is less if we realize what we are doing.

At the risk of distortion, we can look at our effort in this way. Artists and craftsmen distort with their oils and chisels. Everyday photographs capture remembrances and reflect what is known. Occasionally photographs may deliberately distort the obvious and accent the unseen. We call them art instead of snapshots. The following description will distort insofar as it will isolate only one side of life. While it will not tell the entire story, it will be a way of recognizing what is otherwise not easily seen. The following excerpt—adapted from Friedman and Rosenman's work which describes "Type A" behavior (or work-fixation)—may be helpful here:

How do we live when we are work-fixated?

1) We have a habit of explosively accentuating various key words in our ordinary speech even when there is no real need for such accentuation. We also have a tendency to utter the last few words of sentences far more rapidly than the opening words. The vocal explosiveness reflects the aggression we may harbor. Hurrying the ends of sentences mirrors our underlying impatience with spending even the time required for our own speech.

2) We *always* move, walk, and eat rapidly.

3) We feel and exhibit an impatience with the rate at which most events take place. We suffer from this sort of impatience when we find it difficult to restrain ourselves from hurrying the speech of others and resort to the device of saying very quickly over and over again, "Uh huh, uh huh," or "Yes yes, yes yes," to someone who is speaking, unknowingly urging them to hasten the rate of speaking. We also suffer from such impatience when we attempt to finish the sentences of others speaking to us before they can.

   There are other signs of this sort of impatience: when we become *unduly* irritated or even enraged when the car ahead of us in our lane runs at a pace we consider too slow; when we find it anguishing to wait in a line or to wait our turn to be seated at a restaurant; when we find it intolerable to watch others perform tasks we know we can do faster; when we become impatient with ourselves when we are obliged to perform repetitious duties (making out bank deposit slips, writing checks, washing and cleaning dishes, and so on), which are necessary but which take us away from doing things we really have an interest in doing; when we find ourselves hurrying our own reading or always attempting to obtain condensations or summaries of truly interesting and worthwhile literature.

4) When we indulge in *polyphasic* thought or performance, frequently striving to think of or do two or more things simultaneously. For example, if while trying to listen to another person's speech, we persist in continuing to think about an irrelevant subject, we

are indulging in polyphasic thought. Similarly, if while golfing or fishing we continue to ponder our business or professional problems, or if while using an electric razor we attempt also to eat breakfast or drive a car, or if while driving we attempt to dictate letters, we are indulging in polyphasic performance.

5) When we find it *always* difficult to refrain from talking about or bringing the theme of any conversation around to those subjects which especially interest us, and when unable to accomplish this maneuver, we pretend to listen but really remain preoccupied with our own thoughts.

6) When we almost always feel vaguely guilty while we relax or do little for several hours to several days.

7) When we no longer observe the more important and interesting or lovely objects that we encounter in our milieu. For example, if we enter a strange office, store, or home and after leaving any of these places we cannot recall what was in them, we no longer are observing well—or for that matter enjoying life very much.

8) When we do not have any time to spare to become the things worth being, because we are so preoccupied with getting things worth having.

9) When we attempt to schedule more and more in less and less time and in doing so make fewer and fewer allowances for unforeseeable contingencies.

10) When, on meeting other work-fixated persons, instead of feeling compassion for their affliction, we feel compelled to challenge them. No one arouses the aggressive and hostile feelings of one work-fixated person more quickly than another.

11) When we resort to certain characteristic gestures or nervous tics. For example, in conversation, we frequently clench our fists or bang upon a table or pound one fist into the palm of the other hand in order to emphasize a conversational point. Similarly, if the corners of our mouths spasmodically jerk backward or if we habitually clench our jaws or even grind our teeth, we are subject to muscular phenomena suggesting the presence of a continuous struggle.

12) When we believe that whatever success we have enjoyed has been
    due in great part to our ability to get things done faster than others
    and if we are afraid to stop doing everything faster and faster.

13) When we find ourselves increasingly and ineluctably committed
    to translating and evaluating not only our own but also the ac-
    tivities of others in terms of numbers.[1]

None of us is likely to recognize himself or herself in every behavior
that is noted above. But, to the degree that our way of living does cor-
respond to the various descriptions, to that degree there is likelihood
that we live toward the side of life that we have termed work-fixated.

To summarize, we have spoken of work as a project-like stance
characterized by our intention to shape the world about us. We have
referred to work-fixation as an inappropriate project-like way of being
present irrespective of the situation. We are, as it were, stuck in one
way of living. When this occurs and to the degree that it occurs, we
see the world in terms of something to be changed, divide it into what
is useful and not-so-useful, and hold everything and everyone slightly
apart from ourselves in order to move them according to our purpose.
In the process of living in this way we notice that time is experienced
in a special way; we feel its urgency. We are rushed and cannot easily
relax until a project is complete. The difficulty is that as soon as one
task is completed another which must be finished looms on the horizon.
At no time can we rest. Lastly, once we move toward living in a work-
like way, we have to protect what we are building. Since we are building
at all times, we find it necessary to live protectively at all times.

We began our reflections with three examples taken from the lives
of particular individuals. One person was tired with the kind of tiredness
that sleep could not cure. Another desired an elusive intimacy, and the
third spoke of difficulties with trust and belief. Let us return to these
examples in light of our reflections as they have developed.

---

1. M. Friedman and R. Rosenman, *Type A Behavior and Your Heart* (Greenwich: Fawcett—paperback, 1974), pp. 100-102. In quoting we have replaced
the words "Type A Behavior" with "work-fixation" and the personal pronoun
"you" with "we."

"I'm tired most of the time. . . . Taking a nap doesn't relieve my tiredness. . . . I'm tired with the kind of tiredness that sleep can't cure." We know the tiredness that results from digging a hole, moving a cabinet, or cutting a lawn. But all work, not merely physical labor, is tiring. Nothing is changed without effort. Whether we teach a class, keep books, or study, we try to move the world from where we find it. A class resists our efforts to teach; numbers resist our efforts to order them; thoughts resist our efforts to bring them to birth creatively. Even if we are using the word "resist" in an unusual way, it is not unusual to feel the resistance associated with trying to shape the world. To overcome that resistance requires effort and that tires us. In addition, living as a worker requires vigilance. That also necessitates effort but the kind of effort that is more psychic than physical. It is little wonder that we constantly feel tired if we knowingly or unknowingly have reduced all of life to work. While work-fixation is certainly not the cause of all tiredness, it is at least an understandable cause of some.

"I want to be close to someone. . . . Sometimes I dream that I will be able to rest with a loved one. . . . I am not talking about sex. . . . I am talking about closeness." As we work it is necessary to hold the world at a distance in order to change it. Without that distance we will not have the perspective to foresee the next moment on our way toward accomplishing our plans. That is why the worker is always a little detached and why the worker is sometimes thought of in terms of coldness. There is a cunning required in order to work. Work requires that we stand back and apart from what we are doing; a distance develops between ourselves and the world we move.

Suppose it happens that we become workers-at-all. Suppose that there is hardly a moment when we are not working, including apparent moments of relaxation. The isolation can be borne for a time but it is difficult to live that way for years. Very likely it will not be long before we desire to overcome that developed and experienced distance. No wonder a time comes when we desire to be close to someone. Neither is it difficult to understand why we wish to rest with another. What we sometimes call a problem may well be the first sign of our movement away from fixation, even if that motion is clumsy at times. In this sense the person quoted seems so perceptive when he says that he does not think that he is referring to sex when he speaks of his desire to rest with another. The hope he entertains might better be characterized as his desire to look and to be looked upon appreciatively. Such could be the desire of any person caught in work-fixation, married or unmarried, man or woman.

"I don't know if it is a question of belief or not. . . . I think that I am still a believer yet basically distrustful . . . maybe I should say fundamentally distrustful." Again, when we work we have to protect what we are building if we wish to accomplish our task. Our stance tends to be vigilant. The worlds that we build vary. We may construct emotional, physical, or verbal ones. The kind of world is relatively unimportant at this point in our discussion. What is significant to note is that, if we must always form and protect the world, then trust will become an issue for us. It is also conceivable that faith will become an issue insofar as faith necessitates trust.

Each of the difficulties with faith, tiredness, and intimacy can be understood as indications of genuine growth. Our discomfort with ourselves can also be understood as an indication that the world that we held so tightly is beginning to escape our grasp. That escape can announce new life. What was deadened is being enlivened. The misfortune of being always and everywhere a worker is that much of life apart from work is lost. The hands with which we work know only the worker's presence. Lost to the world are the hands of the black woman. That is a tragedy. Both the worker and the world have lost something of their possibilities.

2 Doing Gone Wrong: Work-fixation

Untangling knotted string can be tedious. Unravelling entangled situations can be more so. Work-fixation is an entangled situation that is immensely more complicated and many-faceted than is gnarled string. Yet there is a similarity in the ways that we untangle both. In either instance we proceed one step at a time, working backwards. Once we have accomplished the task we have the opportunity to avoid further knotting by the way in which we handle either the string or ourselves. To understand how we become fixated, let us work sequentially one step at a time much as we would untangle a knotted ball. However, instead of beginning with the knot closest to the end—what might be thought of as the present day—we are going to start with the first knot (infancy) and then work outwards toward the last one (adult life).

Why do we ask the question "How do we fall into work-fixation?" We ask so that we might learn how to move away from it. What is seen can be dealt with more effectively. What is unseen often haunts us. We will start to unravel the entangled situation by describing four possible explanations of the origin of work-fixation. First, let us cite an example of a person who is experiencing great difficulties regarding his job.

He was born in a poverty-stricken Scottish home, but left his family and came to this country at the age of fourteen because there was insufficient food for all of the children. By dint of persistence and hard work, he obtained a B.S. degree, and by gradual stages became one of the technical advisers to a large tire-manufacturing company. Here he came to be held in high respect by the management and the workers; the former recognizing his ability and the latter appreciating his honesty and friendliness. He was an indefatigable worker, arriving at his laboratory very early in the morning and often working late into the night, although this was not required of him in his contract nor expected of him by his superiors. . . .

Although he had always been greatly admired by his superiors, his equals, and his inferiors, he was so busy working that he had no very warm friends among any of them. In fact, he seemed so wrapped up in his work that he was not taken into the confidence of the management as much as he should have been or as much as he wanted to be, but he was the last man on earth to complain about this neglect. . . .

He became depressed. . . . There was nothing either in his private life or in his work to account for it. He was happily married, he was fond of his children, and he had complete economic security. He liked his work and was . . . successful and appreciated. In spite of all this he woke up each morning feeling very much fatigued. . . . He felt incapable of turning out as much work as he should. . . . He felt constantly obliged to force himself to work. . . . He could not dictate letters and would have to write them in longhand, only to be dissatisfied with them and tear them up. . . . Then physical symptoms appeared and he began the rounds of various physicians who attempted to link his depression and work difficulties with some physical cause. He was treated for gastric ulcer, high blood pressure, glandular disorders, allergy, prostate enlargement, and many other things, none of which treatments did him any good.

A crisis was seemingly caused by a change in the company which involved a shift in the direction of his work.

He felt slighted at being told about it only after it had been decided on. He felt that this had been done without a sufficient consideration of whether or not he would be able to function successfully. He interpreted this as an indication that he was not fully appreciated, and supported this idea with the fact that his salary had not been increased in ten years, although the company had made a great deal of money. He had never said a word about this either; but, as he afterwards learned . . . he had been a victim of his own silence, since the management had characteristically assumed that he was satisfied and did not expect any increase. In fact, he had several times said this very thing, and such was his reputation for honesty that no one suspected he was actually being dishonest with himself on this point.

Keeping the difficulties of this man in mind, let us turn to four explanations of work-fixation. After outlining them we will return to this example and reflect upon it in terms of each explanation.

An Explanation

Most individuals are able to work and to love. To be able to do one and not the other represents a cleavage in healthy development. What could lead us to work at the expense of love? It could happen this way.

Maternal love is a love that is given irrespective of our efforts. We have only to be a mother's child. A mother can give a child *all* of her love even though she has many children. Paternal love is different. It is earned. We win such love by effort. All persons, male and female, love in both ways. Mothers love maternally and paternally; so do fathers. This is true even though we usually associate maternal love with mothers, paternal love with fathers.

Suppose that as a child we did not experience maternal love but we did discover a love that we could earn. Given this development it is understandable that we may try to earn maternal love by effort—hardly realizing that we are trying the impossible. We attempt to achieve what cannot be gained by effort. Perhaps it is here that we begin to develop a way of living whereby we strive to obtain the unobtainable. It is at this point that we start on a path that leads us to approach all of life as a task in order to gain a love for which we search but which escapes our grasp.

Understanding the source of our difficulties in this way situates the cause of work-fixation in our earliest life experiences. The sheer accumulation of years in which we have learned to live as we do and the fact that our motivation for living as we do is so hidden make change in later life extraordinarily difficult.

A Second Explanation

Some persons believe that the years of early schooling are the ones during which the seeds of work-fixation are sown. It is particularly between the ages of seven to ten that we learn to work. How? During these years we begin formal schooling and it is then that we first learn to produce, among peers, and largely outside of the protection of the family. For instance, in school there is a task to perform. There are right and wrong answers as well as rewards and punishments for our achievements. At school we learn the feelings associated with success and failure, as well as how to relate to authority apart from the family and in relationship to a task. It is also at school that we learn to live by the clock. There is a time for play and a time for serious work and we must learn to adjust accordingly.

Beyond inciting us to be productive, schooling also teaches us how to work at a job. The habits that we learn in school relative to working side by side with others, living by the clock, experiencing rewards and punishments, successes and failures, and relating to authority within a task-oriented milieu are fundamentally the same realities inherent in most job situations. Schooling forms and readies us as workers.

To understand how we may move toward work-fixation as a result of early school experiences, consider what would happen to us if during those years we learned that we were good if we succeeded, bad if we failed. None of us, especially as a child, wants to feel that he or she is bad or that he or she deserves punishment. It is conceivable that we would try to avoid such feelings by learning to work determinedly and steadily. As youngsters we might even learn to avoid the sting of failure by working unusually hard for those around us. No one wants to condemn hard work. Having others recognize our efforts effectively eliminates their criticism and merits for us the words we so desperately want to hear: "You're a good boy, Johnny." "You're a good girl, Mary."

Learning to associate goodness and badness with our work need not have been conscious during childhood. To the degree that we were unaware of establishing these associations, they assume greater or lesser importance in our adult life. We only know that we feel uncomfortable when others see us resting. On hearing their footsteps we look for something to do in order to appear busy. Caught relaxing or enjoying an activity apart from work, we feel the need to justify ourselves. The ability to relax comfortably and to enjoy life ends up being restricted by our needs to avoid punishment and to be praised.

As with the first explanation of work-fixation, if these are the dynamics involved in our living fixatedly, to change our way of living as adults is difficult. Deeply ingrained patterns of living learned early in life are not changed easily.

A Third Explanation

All of us need to feel valuable. Many of us feel that we have few ways to achieve recognition, confirmation, a feeling of worth, and a sense of value apart from proving ourselves in a work-like way. Often, a job serves as an arena for work.

The job world holds before us the possibility of becoming valuable. "If I become a doctor, missionary, mayor, mother, or priest," we say to ourselves, "I will be doing something worthwhile." What we mean but do not say is that we will also feel valuable as a result. However, no job, of itself, provides a sense of value. Two persons may become nurses. One finds giving needles a rewarding type of involvement. The job awakens a sense of its significance as well as of one's personal value. Another person doing the same job finds giving needles dehumanizing. "Any machine can do what I do." What our cultural incentives to work fail to make explicit is a difference between recognizing our valuableness and achieving it by the job that we perform. The difference is important. Failure to recognize it can lead toward work-fixation.

If we have no sense of our valuableness, we set about trying to build ourselves through the job that we have. Consider the way in which two persons approach the work of teaching. One person, lacking a sense of value, chooses to teach in order to become valuable. She uses the job to gain affection or to prove her worth. Students become the means she employs to build her sense of value. While it looks as though she is involved with others, her eyes are really on herself.

A second person may approach the same job differently. Having a sense of her own value, she can be forgetful of herself long enough to be attentive to the work at hand. Her eyes tend to be on the students more than on herself. In the process of attentiveness to teaching others, she may be rewarded with confirmation of her valuableness but she is not particularly looking for it.

The difference between the two workers is that one woman uses her work for personal growth, whereas the other merely recognizes how valuable she is in the midst of activity. It is the first woman who illustrates the way in which an unfulfilled need can lead us to work at everything, even ourselves.

A Fourth Explanation

Overwork can lead toward work-fixation. Drive the same path long enough and you form a little road. Continue to use the same tracks and it is nearly impossible to avoid or to escape the ruts you have made. Overwork can depress and deform. It leads toward work-fixation by wearing one down to the point of exhaustion.

All work tires. While we are not machines, working requires an expenditure of energy beyond which we cannot reach without deforming ourselves. Exhaustion and depression accompany overwork. The younger we are the easier it is to bounce back if we do overwork. Bodily rest is all that is needed if the exhaustion and depression are largely physical. A different activity that brings satisfaction is enough to relieve psychological exhaustion. Reading, a walk in the woods, play, or worship may rekindle our waning spirit. But as we become older and disregard the boundary between work and overwork, we are worn in a way that permanently deforms. We grow accustomed to no other way of living than a work-like way. There is a point at which we become so habituated to the work stance that rest and play no longer bring refreshment.

The move toward work-fixation takes place gradually. The resiliency of youth veils what is happening to us. Our situation bears some similarity to the abuse of alcohol when we are young. It is easy to recover if we overindulge. However, time makes change difficult. The same is true with overwork. In middle and later years discouragement and depression are so pervasive that we do not have the energy to change.

There is nothing subtle about overwork. We usually realize when we have gone too far. The problem lies in feeling that we cannot stop. There is still too much unfinished that needs to be done and too much asked of us that we cannot avoid doing.

Competency may entice us into this situation. It is the competent person to whom we turn when something needs to be done. He or she is the one who immediately recognizes needs and who can do what has to be done better and more efficiently than many others. It is not long before the talented person both sees and is asked to do more than is humanly possible.

But competency alone is not the culprit. It is when competency exists side by side with unfulfilled needs that problems arise. If we have unusually strong needs to please others, to appear generous or self-sacrificing or if we are *pushed* to excel, to be in charge, or to have power and if at the same time we are highly talented, we are particularly vulnerable to overwork. There is almost no way to avoid it. We want to be helpful and we can do many things well. The difficulty is that it is not long before we lose our vibrancy in the midst of too much to do. Called "burnout," this problem exists among many professionals.

If competency is one way that we sometimes move toward overwork, incompetency—or what might better be termed disparity between our talents and our employment—is another way. All persons are talented. Different activities require different talents. If we are involved throughout the day in an activity for which we do not have the talents, we will have to exert an extraordinary amount of effort and at considerable cost to ourselves to achieve what may be practically beyond our abilities. In this situation, a sense of frustration is high and the likelihood of failure almost certain. If economic necessity, a need to save face, or any other need grips us in the activity over a long period of time, overwork easily results.

Unspoken philosophies may also move us toward overwork. Without saying as much, we still often convey such convictions as: "To be busy is good; to be idle is bad"; or, "Those who do more are better than those who do less." We seldom voice these thoughts but sometimes live by them, and they can press us into otherwise dutiful and purposeful activities in unthinking ways. We feel uncomfortable during moments of legitimate rest when those around us are working hard or when our own projects are still incomplete. Though we may not *think* so, we *feel* that there is something wrong with rest when there is work to be done. Seldom do we feel that there is something wrong with work when there is need for rest. More often than not, and irrespective of what it does to us as persons, it is even praiseworthy to work when rest is needed. Our unspoken philosophies influence us in pervasive ways.

Perhaps there are as many ways to become involved in overwork as there are persons in varying situations. The ones that we have identified are frequent and also varied in the ways in which they manifest themselves. But there are other explanations as well. Some are as self-evident as economic necessity. Others are as forcefully felt as the pressure that people can exert upon us by the strength of their personalities, pushing us beyond the limits of our abilities, endurance, and desires. Still other ways are as subtle as the competitiveness inherent in living together and leading us to outdo one another. Husbands and wives, friends, neighbors, and fellow workers can all lead us toward overwork by their accomplishments and our felt deficiencies. Maybe the saddest but not the most uncommon development is when work restricts us to such an extent that we have nothing better to do. "Having nothing better to do" is the really sad aspect of what has occurred because it robs our activity of any liveliness. If the activity is a job, we start to move from bed to table to job and back to bed, as if in a circle; and our death, when it occurs, will be that of a machine rather than of a person.

To summarize, overwork leads to work-fixation through the deprivation of experience apart from work and by the deformation of personality that results from unrelieved exhaustion.

Now, let us return to our example. Recall that the man was born in poverty, left home at an early age, and that by hard work he slowly advanced to a responsible position in his company. He went to work early in the morning and stayed until late at night. We remember him as conscientious and responsible. Then, seemingly without reason and in the midst of success, he began to develop various illnesses in addition to an inability to work. Do the four explanations of the origins of work-fixation help us to understand the difficulties this man is finding?

In terms of the first explanation, the source of his difficulties apparently lies in infancy. We do know that his life was difficult as a child and that in adulthood he suffers from a feeling of not being appreciated. Appreciation is the kernel of maternal love. Perhaps he never experienced such love as a child. It is true that he earned the affection and admiration of those around him. He knew how to gain paternal love. Could it be that throughout his adult life he has been trying to earn maternal love by sheer effort? If this be the case, it explains to some degree his present crisis. He may be attempting to gain a love for which he searches but which escapes his grasp.

His difficulties might also stem from experiences at school. While not denying that these difficulties may have begun earlier in life, it is also conceivable that early school experiences set him on a path toward work-fixation. We know that schooling must have been especially significant for him. It was through schooling that he rose beyond his poverty-stricken milieu and by persistent hard work obtained his college degree. It was the same kind of diligent effort that enabled him to advance on the job. He had to learn to discipline himself early in life, to live gracefully among his peers, and to achieve outside of the protection of the family, if for no other reason than that he was away from home, on his own, and responsible for his own livelihood.

He was almost compelled to avoid failure and to rise above what he knew to be his past. To fail would have meant to return to what he had escaped. All would certainly have praised him for his efforts to excel. On his part he would have had to learn to avoid the sting of failure by demonstrating unusually hard work. Perhaps during those years in school he learned to live in a way that limited all of life to what could be achieved. For him as a child, it may have been a question of what *had* to be achieved rather than what *could* be achieved. Almost through circumstances beyond his control, a side of life beyond achievement was closed to him. It is understandable, then, that later in life when relatively secure, he would find it useless to live as he was living but yet *be unable* to do otherwise. He stands between two worlds: one that has become lifeless, and another in which he does not yet know how to live.

A third explanation can be offered along the lines made by a psychiatrist who helped this man through the crisis. It is this:

> The nucleus of the problem was that for this man the sublimative function of work was overtaxed. The feeling of not being appreciated and of not getting his deserts began, of course, in his childhood, which had been a very hard and bitter period. For some years a successful method of sublimating these resentments held them in check and incognito; ultimately they became too strong and threatened to overwhelm the protective barrier. It was then that the emergency defense of depression, self-depreciation, and physical illness were called upon — and this is what we see as the illness.[1]

We can also understand his difficulties in terms of overwork. Overwork depresses and deforms. It leads to work-fixation by wearing us down to the point of exhaustion. He worked hard and for long hours each day. He was also competent. Others admired him for his abilities and talents. Competency combined with strongly felt and unfulfilled needs often leads to overwork. He had extremely strong needs to excel as well as to appear self-sacrificing. Such a combination could conceivably have pushed him toward overwork. Also, the way that he worked kept others at a distance. Few persons would bother him because he seemed so involved in his job. Given the way that he lived, he could easily have reached a point where he had "nothing better to do" than to work. With that motivation, even his job would have lacked spontaneity.

Each of these explanations is believable. To some degree each has been substantiated by the fact that we have used them knowingly and/or unknowingly to try to help one another as doctors, co-workers, clergy, and friends. Generally speaking, however, the help that we provide for

---

1. K. Menninger and J. L. Menninger, *Love Against Hate* (New York: Harcourt, Brace, 1947), pp. 141-145.

one another is short-lived. Seldom do we rid ourselves of the difficulties that we experience; instead, we learn to live with them. We tell one another that it is but a question of adjusting.

Without neglecting the truth of the explanations already given, let us look at our difficulties, not from the perspective of those who have difficulties with work but from the perspective of those whom we might call vocation-loving individuals. These are the people who do not seem to need to get away from their work as most of us do. Sometimes it is even incongruous to think of them as needing a traditional vacation. Who among us would not find it surprising to hear that Mother Teresa of Calcutta went on a skiing holiday? Yet the curious fact seems to be that she is not particularly drained though she must certainly become tired. Vocation-loving individuals seem to have an unusual reserve of energy. Oftentimes they seem unable, or at least feel it unnecessary, to separate work from leisure. Let us think about these things for a moment. The lives of such persons provide an insight into work-fixation and difficulties with faith, tiredness, and intimacy.

Most of us divide activities into those that we have to do and those that we want to do. The time for one is work; the time for the other is leisure. We refer to a division that is felt rather than reasoned. Vocation-loving individuals do not seem to experience life in this way. Distinguishing between work and leisure tends to be unnecessary because what they *have* to do and what they *want* to do are one and the same. That simple distinction has far-reaching consequences.

Take the lives of two mothers as illustrative. One woman conceives and welcomes her pregnancy. Another conceives but does not want a child. These two women live in vastly different worlds. The first woman we will call vocation-loving because what she wants and what is asked of her are synonymous. The second woman could represent any of us who live torn between what we have to do and what we want to do. She finds herself carrying a child but she does not want to be a mother. There is a disharmony in her life because what is asked of her is other than what she wants. As a consequence her life is fragmented.

The pain involved in carrying, bearing, and rearing a child is indicative of what happens to the two women and to each of us. Both women experience pain. There is no way to avoid it. For one woman there is a context in which to accept the pain; she wants to be a mother. The second woman who does not want the child also experiences pain, but for her it is a constant reminder of what she does not want. Every moment of pain produces a reminder of what is unwanted. Frustration is sure to result.

We have already mentioned some ways to explain the origin of work-fixation. Could we not speak of its cause in a more simple manner? Could work-fixation be the consequence of living without leisure? If experientially we divide the moments of each day into work and leisure, and if leisure disappears from life, work is all that will remain. If this is true, the pivotal question is how and why leisure disappears. The lives of vocation-loving individuals can help us see how leisure, understood as a spacious way of living, can disappear.

Leisure will disappear to the degree that we do not do what we want to do. That thought has to be clarified and will be as we continue. But the insight can be phrased another way: that we become work-fixated when all of life becomes something that we have to do. Following this line of reasoning, many of the difficulties found in the workaday world can be said to stem from the disharmony between what we want to do and what we have to do.

What does it mean to "want" to do something? It refers to something that is embraced, to a choice. We do not intend to use the word in the sense of "I want to do that," which can be understood as "I would 'like' that." This use of the word is synonymous with feelings of pleasantness. Our use of the word implies that we may want something without particularly liking it. A woman may want to be a mother but not like the pain involved. Nonetheless she can fully choose to be a mother. We desire to use the word "want" in reference to an *ability to choose wholeheartedly.*

By "having to do" we mean that *something is asked of us.* Not in the sense that we "should" do this or that we "ought" to do that. Such words usually refer to external commands. They have their origin apart from us as individuals and they can become tyrannical. When we speak of something being asked of us, we refer to an invitation that arises because of a harmony between us and our situation and not apart from us as individuals. Instead of restricting, the choice of what is asked of us ultimately frees and leads to a sense of comfortableness. An example might be helpful.

The woman whose experience we are going to cite is considering a job change. Her two children are away at college and she wants to be involved outside of the home in a way that is helpful to others and interesting for her. Before marriage she was a pharmacologist and nurse. She worked for five years as a druggist until her first child was born during her second year of marriage.

> Two of my friends are encouraging me to work as a nurse. They say it is more human than working in a lab and making pills. They also say that there is a need for nurses. They are right about that. The paper is filled with help-wanted ads for nurses. My husband is great. He says that whatever I do I'll do well. . . .
>
> . . . I must say that pharmacology is more interesting to me than nursing. Even though I am a nurse I don't think that I am particularly good at it. I feel that it is something I can do—like cooking a frozen meal. I am a good druggist and I enjoy it even though most people don't see that kind of work as interesting. . . .
>
> . . . The problem is that I feel selfish. That's what it all boils down to. I enjoy being a druggist but I feel selfish for leaning in that direction when I know damn well that the hospital needs nurses. I'm not sure what I should do.

None of us is sure. We do not know the woman who has spoken, nor do we know her situation in its full complexity. Even if we did, we would not know what decision should be made. Each of us is always and everywhere responsible, and all decisions have an uncertainty about them. However, her experience can illustrate the difference between something that is asked of us and something that we ought to do. We conjecture that the woman feels the urge to be a nurse as a *should* and the inclination to be a druggist as something that is *asked* of her.

Why? Because of what she tells us about herself in the situation. We know that she wants to make a sound decision. That is why she has asked the advice of others. We also know that she receives unmistakable advice. Become a nurse, her friends say, it is more humanizing than being a druggist. They also remind her of the need for nurses. Phrased in this way there is hardly a decision to be made. She almost has to decide upon nursing. Who wants to choose what is less than human? Who wants to be selfish?

That is the way that *shoulds* work. They are coercive. They move us to decide by being so strongly felt that we can hardly avoid the direction in which they push. They overpower most other feelings. Even a scream cannot be heard when a siren wails. *Shoulds* resemble sirens. In the instance described, the woman is moved to overlook her own inclinations, interests, talents, and dreams. Yet the feelings associated with these latter movements are the ones that form a significant part of the reality to which we refer when we speak of the need to be attentive to what is asked of us in life.

In effect, if we live by *shoulds* we disregard ourselves. We remain predominantly sensitive to the objectified needs of the world apart from us. To continue to disregard our talents, interests, and dreams is to reduce involvement to duty. In the process, work loses its liveliness. That is unfortunate. Using the example of the woman about to choose a new job, it is conceivable that her decision to become a nurse under the pressure of *shoulds* will not enhance the nursing profession with the presence of a lively and interested worker. Neither will she be of help to those whom she could have served effectively as a caring druggist. Nor will she have helped herself.

Even so, there is no condemnation. Not everything is bleak. Uninformed decisions can lead to places for which we are grateful at a later moment. That is the mystery and beauty of human existence. However, just because uninformed decisions may blossom in unexpected ways, this need not encourage us to live by them.

Informed decisions do not by-pass conflict and obviate all tension. Choosing to become a druggist may involve living in a way contrary to the advice of close friends. That can be uncomfortable. Choosing to become a druggist may also awaken feelings of regret at not being able to be a nurse. Such feelings linger because the worlds we have not chosen will never be known, and we are almost bound to wonder about the roads not taken. What we do know are the worlds that our decisions have opened, and there is a great likelihood that we will be grateful for those worlds if we strive to live faithful to what is asked of us. . . . All of this by way of saying that there is a difference between being compelled by *shoulds* and being sensitive to what is asked of us in life.

It can clarify the distinctions that we have been making between "shoulds," "oughts," "choices," "likes," "what is asked of us," and "what we want" to say that each person has a destiny. There is a task that "calls for" each of us. Objectively speaking, there are *many* tasks that can be chosen; there are many possible paths to follow in life. Yet at the same time the many possible tasks that are open to us have a way of narrowing down. "The" task is one for which we are particularly suited, like a key for a lock. It is the task with which we have a mutual compatibility as in a good marriage. There is something about being made for each other even though there may be many possible "others."

> What happens then to the one who denies this unique responsibility? who doesn't listen to his call-note? or who can't hear at all any more? Here we can certainly talk about intrinsic guilt, or intrinsic unsuitability, like a dog trying to walk on his hind legs, or a poet trying to be a good businessman, or a businessman trying to be a poet. It just doesn't fit; it doesn't suit; it doesn't belong. One must respond to one's fate or one's destiny or pay a heavy price. One must yield to it; one must surrender to it. One must permit one's self to be chosen.[2]

Returning to our line of thought, how do we become work-fixated? It is by forgetting how to live leisurely. How does that happen? By not allowing ourselves to be chosen. We forget to listen to what is asked of us. As a consequence, our lives are split between work and leisure — work being what we have to do, leisure encompassing what we want to do. From this point onward we have two choices. We can try to safeguard one world from the other or we can choose to avoid the conflict by accenting one at the expense of the other. This results in our working all of the time or in being unable to work at all. It is the heavy price we pay for failing to listen to what is asked of us in life.

Knowing what is asked is never as clearly grasped as a fact is. Neither is it unknown in quite the way that something escapes our comprehension.

---

2. Abraham Maslow, *Eupsychian Management* (Homewood, Ill.: Dorsey Press, 1965), p. 10.

There comes a time when we realize that we have to limit, arrange, and participate in life with the prospect of death before us. It is then that we have an almost undeniable realization of what is asked of us in life. Such a realization changes us. The change is not always a conscious one. Neither is it something that happens only in old age. It can occur in youth. It is always a sign of adulthood.

Does this explanation of how we become work-fixated make sense relative to difficulties with tiredness, faith, and intimacy?

It does in terms of tiredness. If we find ourselves having to do what we do not really want to do during many hours of every day, then it is understandable how we will feel a pervasive tiredness. We will have to exert continual effort to push ourselves through each day, aware or unaware of the effort required. No amount of bodily rest will relieve the tiredness that results from having to muster the energy to push ourselves through life. This is true even on the level of employment. The following words are those of a child welfare worker who is misplaced in her job.

> All I've had to do for the past six days is to write a single report. Every time I put the paper in the typewriter I get sleepy. I keep putting off and putting off what I know has to be done. I can never forget it and I can never do it. I used to be able to write six or seven of them in a morning. Now I've got to push myself to write one every couple of days.

The explanation of difficulties with sexuality as they stem from work and leisure is worth considering when we think of the implications of the split between what we want and what we have to do.

> When I'm frustrated I masturbate. It's that simple. I'm not saying anything other than that's the way it is. What is surprising to me is that ever since I came out here I'm not inclined to do it.

Let us try to solve the problems involved in dividing life-experience between work and leisure by opting to live all of life in a work-like way. In the process of living as if all is work, we forget how to live. All time and all space are for work and in terms of work. It is not long before we are run down by the task at hand. Frustrated, we seek relief in masturbation.

Suppose, however, that we move to another situation in which time and space are used differently. This could be caused by going into a hospital, attending a workshop, or taking a vacation. The new use of time and space could easily account for the reason we no longer experience difficulty with, let us say, masturbation. Our lives, which were slightly distorted by the way in which we lived, have found a new balance.

Could such a change merely be the short-lived effect of new and absorbing interests? Yes. An adage reminds us that if we pack a messy suitcase we will arrive with one. A simple change of place solves nothing of itself. But a change of place can teach us a new use of time and space and a new way to live.

It can offer an opportunity to learn about ourselves.

With this in mind it is conceivable that some of our difficulties with sexuality could stem from the way that we live rather than from deeply felt and unresolved developmental difficulties. That is not to say, however, that such developmental difficulties are not due partly to the way we use space and time in adult life. Rather, the way we use space and time influences the way we experience life and may cause problems which at first hardly seemed related.

Practically speaking, where do these reflections take us? What questions arise? What directions are indicated? Until now our strokes have been broad. We need to focus more sharply by turning our thoughts directly to the issue of leisure.

3 The Eclipse of Leisure

How can we avoid work-fixation? Is it a matter of finding time for leisure? If so, why is trying to get away so difficult? Even when we do find some leisure time it does not always refresh.

I had a peculiar experience the other day. I had just spent the last six days at the ocean with friends. The time was wonderful. I ate well, slept soundly, and relished the color that returned to my face. The peculiar experience is this. As soon as I opened the door to my office I had the feeling that I had never been away. I can't tell you how lethargic I felt. It was as if those days at the ocean hadn't existed. It all happened in an instant, even before I let go of the door knob. Today nothing remains of my vacation except the knowledge that I took one and a little bit of suntan.

In our fixation, could we have forgotten leisure? We know that what looks like work is not always work. Could what looks like leisure sometimes be work?

Speaking about leisure can be as difficult as speaking about work. One explanation lies in our varied use of the word. We speak of leisure as a time for something, as an activity, and as an attitude. Let us look at each of these ways. Where our reflections will lead us may not be clear at this point, but we hope they will help clarify the problems associated with work-fixation.

Frequently we use the word "leisure" to refer to a time. It is the time that we do what we want to do, as distinguished from the time to do what we have to do. Often enough the having-to-do is drudgery while leisure is associated with the pleasant side of life. Using the words "work" and "leisure" in this way reflects our everyday experience that work and leisure are separate and often conflicting types of activity.

Besides speaking of leisure as a period of time, we also use it to refer to the activities in which we can be leisurely involved. Hobbies, playing, vacationing, and things that we do for relaxation are such activities. When using the word in this manner, what is leisure for one person may not be for another. Tending a garden is leisure activity for one person, work for another.

Lastly, we speak of leisure as an attitude that affects the pace of what we are doing. We walk leisurely. Many of us would like to be able to work and eat leisurely. Just as leisure can refer to a time apart, it can also designate the pace at which we do something.

Each way in which we use the word has some relationship with time. How curious that we do not refer to leisure in terms of space. Both space *and* time root us in life. To forget either is to risk distortion. Could it be that we have forgotten a whole side of life—the spatial side—while living as if all is work? If a number of us were to live this way nothing would appear unusual, simply because we would all be living alike. The possibility may appear far-fetched, but it is at least worth considering.

Historically, we have reason to believe that whole areas of life can escape awareness. Apparently it occurred in the nineteenth century when the sexual dimension of living went unrecognized by many persons. At least this was Freud's contention. We also have reason to believe that it takes time to recognize realities that have always been present but which we have not seen. Art history offers a significant example. It took centuries before artists began to see and to develop techniques to paint in terms of the third dimension of depth. Once a few persons recognized depth and developed techniques to paint what they saw, all were led to see what was not previously noticed. Today, we even wonder why everyone could not see what is now so obvious to all. To give another example, once we are made aware of an idiosyncrasy—perhaps the overuse of a certain word—we catch ourselves using the word time and again even though we were previously unaware of the habit.

Returning to our theme of leisure, let us see if we can speak of it in terms of space. All we have to do is to isolate an activity when we live "leisurely." At such a time we do not have to consciously remind ourselves to slacken our pace; we do it naturally. Let us consider a visit to a museum. When walking through a museum we do not have to say to ourselves, "Now we are going to try to walk slowly!" That is unnecessary. Why is it that there are places where we instinctively relax the pace at which we live and other places where we hurry? Can we say anything about them in terms of space?

First, normally in the places where we slow down, there is a lot of space. Most galleries are large rooms. The ceilings are high, the floors bare, the walls white, and if there is any furniture at all it is usually a bench in the middle of the room. Its smallness accents rather than fills space. Usually it looks lost and almost out of place in the gallery. The paintings accent space by the way that they are hung. Many more could be placed in the space left empty between paintings. Even lighting contributes to the sense of space. The lights that are present are usually hidden and they illumine the paintings rather than the room.

Something else is noticeable. Besides the slow pace of those who are present, it is also evident that when we speak in the gallery we do so softly and in short rather than involved sentences. We say, "I like that!" "I don't like that!" Even children tend to walk slowly in galleries— often without the constraining hands of their parents.

We can compare such a place with another where we tend to be present in a hurried way. Consider a crowded airport. Most of us rush through it. We are on our way somewhere. There is a sense of movement if not excitement about the situation. Children chase one another. There are outbreaks of laughter and occasional teary eyes. Adults try to keep children in order without much success. Some parents try to quiet the children by distracting them; others try physical restraints and spankings. We can hear: "Stand up." "Be good." "Stop that." "Come here." Most of us would say that words that come to mind to describe older airports are "noise," "hurry," "frustration," and "crowding." When we look around, especially when we notice parents with children, we can see that effort is required to keep an eye on them. It is also evident that the experience is a tiring one for all. Neither parents nor children seem to win.

In addition to the quickened pace of the airport, the noise level is noticeably greater. Words are not minimal as in the museums. There is much talk and people often speak to one another at the same time.

The worlds of museums and airports are remarkably different. If crowding characterizes airports or other places where we tend to rush, space characterizes the museums where we slow down. What is the effect of space? If we are too close, too crowded, with too much to see, we quicken our pace. If there is enough space and it is arranged in such a way as to facilitate noticing what is around us, our pace slows. Slowing down does not seem to be a question of doing so in order to notice, as much as it seems to be a result of involvement. We have to be careful about our reflections here. There is more to a slow or fast pace than physical space. We can be as hurried in spacious airports as we can be slowed in small museums where space is at a premium. However, let us leave clarifications for later and pursue the relationship between space and leisure a little farther.

What is curious about the example of the museum is that there is little need to *try* to slow down. We do so almost without realizing it. Gone is the need for effort. When we consider leisure solely from the vantage point of time, it seems as though we try to become leisurely by will-power. We say to ourselves in so many differing ways, "I must try to slow down a little." Or, to take the example beyond the museums and airports, we tell ourselves—and make firm resolutions—to eat more slowly. Our efforts are about as successful as the efforts of parents to control their children in crowded places. However, when we consider leisure in terms of space, we get a fresh perspective on the difficulty we have trying to slow down. How do people in museums begin to move leisurely? By becoming involved. How do they become involved? By having enough distance to notice but not so much as to be detached. Besides implying time, leisure implies space as well; and attention to it is important.

Something else is suggested by considering leisure in terms of space. Busyness and a hurried pace might just as well reflect non-involvement as involvement. We say this because it seems as though our pace is spontaneously slowed when we are involved. Stated another way we could say that busyness may be the result of being either too close or too distanced from life. Hurry could be the flurry that mirrors non-involvement. However, in the midst of busyness it is probably difficult to see that the problem is related to space, just as it is difficult for parents and children to listen to one another in a crowded and bustling airport, where there might be almost too much to see at one time. Each of us has to find a space in which to stand. Figuratively speaking, we have to find a gallery. That may happen when we go to the mountains, walk the beach, or enter an empty church. It could also be when we close a door. The necessity is to find it in the city, among friends, on the job, and in all of daily life.

Given these reflections, how do we wish to speak of leisure? We want to say that it is a *spacious way of living that involves time.* This is a difficult way of speaking. We do not have the words in our vocabulary that refer to leisure as a spatial as well as temporal reality. All of our words are time-oriented. Leisure has come to mean unoccupied time, free time, time at our disposal, or the time to do something at our convenience. By the latter we mean "when we have time." Lastly, as we have already noted, we use the word to designate the pace of activity which, again, is in terms of time.

Actually, our language perpetuates the difficulty of trying to live leisurely. It furthers the distortion inasmuch as we have not developed a vocabulary that reflects the role of space in leisure. This situation is somewhat similar to our awakened sensitivity to women in our culture. We now recognize how language reflects attitudes toward women, and yet we find it difficult to change our attitudes simply because we do not have the words to help us. The words that we do have tend to perpetuate our difficulties. The same is true when we speak of leisure. We do not have a vocabulary to use in order to help us see it in terms of space as well as of time. So when we refer to leisure as a spacious way of living that involves time, the words seem particularly difficult to comprehend and to make practical. Hopefully, the uneasiness we may feel in speaking in this way will be short-lived.

We can acquire more ease by developing the thought and searching for words to understand our experience better. Think back to the three experiences with which we began our reflections to see if they are understandable in terms of space. The persons quoted spoke of difficulties with faith, intimacy, and tiredness. Could those difficulties arise as leisure is eclipsed in the process of living in a non-spacious way?

Suppose leisure is accurately termed a spacious way of living. Suppose, also, that we begin to live hurriedly because we are uninvolved rather than over-involved and that this hurriedness results from standing either too close or too distanced from life. If this developed there would be a child within us whom we must try to control. We would constantly have to say to ourselves, "Slow down." "Be quiet." We know from experience that such effort meets with little success. The same tiredness that parents feel could be ours as well. In this sense it is understandable that the kind of tiredness that sleep cannot cure could be the expected consequence of living without leisure.

To stand too far from or too close to life means that we would not notice what is before us. Though hurried, we would be uninvolved. It would be like running through a museum while never noticing what was there. There would never be a time for our eyes to catch or be caught by wonderment. We would never know the experience of resting appreciatively. In fact, if we lived fixatedly in a non-spacious way, the entire appreciative side of life would be diminished. Given this situation, it is understandable that we would yearn to rest with someone, and we would be speaking not so much in terms of sex as in terms of desiring an appreciative and caring eye.

If our hurried ways reveal that we no longer stand in a place to notice, then we are tending to dull the receptive side of life. Giving is easy; receiving difficult. To the degree that this occurs it is also understandable that trust and faith would present special difficulties since both faith and trust presuppose creative receptivity to others.

We began this chapter by asking ourselves if moving away from work-fixation is merely a question of finding time for leisure. It now appears that it is not. While we have not yet considered how we might help ourselves as well as one another, we have been led to a few insights that are likely to be helpful as we continue our reflections. First, we have seen that leisure has a spatial as well as a temporal dimension.

We have spoken of it as a spacious way of living that involves time. Second, we can think of that spatial dimension as a place to stand, a stance that is distanced enough to see, yet close enough for intimacy. It is a psychological as well as physical space to which we refer. Third, we have noted that leisure is a reflection of how we are involved. In this sense, leisure is a characteristic of involvement rather than something that must first be achieved or else wrested from our duties in the workaday world. Finally, we are led to believe that our efforts to live leisurely are likely more informed when we look for ways to facilitate involvement rather than to strengthen our willful efforts to slow down.

From what we have said it follows that we look at leisure from a particular perspective. We are referring to it in terms of spacious living. We do not speak of the fact that we may spend too much time in an office, kitchen, or workshop. Neither do we refer to the need for more leisure time or to the need to find interesting leisure-time activities. We do not praise the value of *being* at the expense of the value of *doing*, or vice versa. What we are speaking about is leisure as a way of living and as a component of all involvement whether the activity is a job, game, prayer, or sleep. If there is an observation that we wish to accent, it is this: that despite all our activity, the reality seems to be that we are under- rather than overinvolved. Our busyness reflects a condition of being scattered. The remembrance of the slowed pace of the museum people speaks convincingly of what is missing. We need to be slowed by involvement.

4 Mistaken Solutions

We are at the point of considering how to escape living in a work-fixated way. A frequent attempt, but hardly a solution, is to substitute one fixation for another. For instance, instead of work we can substitute alcohol. With time we may be unable to work, and it may look as if we have moved from our work-fixated ways; but the underlying way that we live remains the same: we maintain the addictive stance. Before speaking of an informed avoidance of work-fixation, let us first illustrate a false solution.

When we fall into work-fixation we settle for a single-dimensioned way of living. We have only one way to relate to the worlds about us. We say "fixated" to stress that we cannot shift out of the stance of a worker. Addiction is another way to speak about work-fixation. The word "addiction" is formed from two Latin words, *ad* and *dicere,* which when combined mean "to speak to." In addiction we allow only one aspect of reality to speak to us. If we are addicted to work, we live sensitively to anything within the work sphere; anything apart from it escapes our awareness and appreciation. There are many ways of being addicted; work is only one of them.

The move from work-fixation to a more relaxed openness to the world is often confused with merely a change in the object of our fixation while maintaining the same stance. Substituting one addiction for another is frequent simply because the shift is accomplished so easily. Also, we appear so different as we shift addictions that the change often disguises our sameness.

To illustrate changing one addiction for another let us fantasize for a moment. We will create two men. Let them be accomplished administrators. Playfully, and maybe a little unfairly, we will make the

51

men rigid and noticeably abrupt in the way they relate with others. They will be noted for being orderly, punctual, and responsible. We will also make them highly efficient. They are fair and balanced in their judgments. They work long hours each day, often six and seven days a week, and their offices run smoothly because of them. There are no surprises with the men we are creating; they are steady fellows, almost predictable in every detail. Because these men are detached, organized, and controlled, others count on them but do not seem close to them.

While our description does not indicate being fixated, let us presume that they are. The first man speaks after eleven years of administration and during a time of unexplained crisis.

You know, I never had a drink until I was twenty-six. I even remember the first one; it was a whiskey sour. I shudder when I think about it today. It was like drinking a bowl of fruit. It wasn't long before I moved away from them and discovered manhattans. True, they are a little sweet, but they're nothing like whiskey sours. I like them even today. We used to have manhattans before supper each day. I must say that I grew to look forward to them. That was three years ago. I remember the first time that I tried a martini, and now looking back I can see why I liked them. They're much drier. Also, it's easy enough to make a good one. I like one each evening before supper. They relax me and I enjoy the social aspect of being with others.

Yes, I do laugh at the time that I was into martinis. Today I prefer scotch and a little water. Not too much water, just enough. The first time that I tasted scotch I thought it tasted like aspirin. Today, I say thank God for aspirin. True, I do take two drinks at night, sometimes three, but that is all. I have one or two before bed just to relax me.

No, you are wrong. I don't really have a problem with alcohol. Yesterday and the day before as well, I did have a shot before going over to school, but that is unusual. I was careful to take vodka so people wouldn't know. I feel much better after a drink or two and I think that others think that I am the better for it. Before, they used to call me a little uptight. Some say that I'm over-conscientious and that I can't relax. Whatever they think, the fact is that I know that after I have a few drinks I feel warmer and closer to others. That's the truth. Remember last night? That was tremendous. I remember putting my arm around that woman with whom I've had so much trouble. We sang together. I usually dislike being around her. Last night I didn't. See what I mean? Drink helps me.

These are the words of the first man whom we have created. Now, let us turn to a second man. This time, instead of having him speak, we will listen to the way that others speak about him in his moment of unexplained change.

(a comment)

I don't know what's happened to him, but he sure has changed. It seems to me that ever since he came back from that workshop he's not been the same. He used to be over in that office six and sometimes seven days a week. Lord only knows what he did all that time, but he was certainly there. I'm beginning to think that his heart really isn't in this place anymore.

(a comment)

I like what is happening to him. I think he's letting his hair grow a little. Yesterday I heard that he has started to grow a mustache! I like it. Before I always had the devil in me to reach out and mess up that hair of his which is so perfect all the time.

(a comment)

You may like his changing but I don't. Twice I gave him memos and both times he's forgotten about them.

(a comment)

Did you see him last night? I never knew that he wore anything other than conservative greys and blacks.

(a comment)

Am I ever envious of that fellow! He looks like he's lost thirty pounds. Healthfood nut or not, I've got to hand it to him. Look at the way he's out there jogging. I don't know where he gets the discipline.

(a comment)

I don't like the guy. This place has fallen apart and he's the trouble. I hardly recognize him and I don't like his new-found personalism. If he'd stop being so damn compassionate and make a decent decision, I'd be happier and this place would be the better for it.

(a comment)

I hear that he's going to get another job or go back to the university.

In our make-believe world we have created two men who have tried to move from work-fixation. At first they were highly efficient, responsible persons who worked long hours each day. Even though a little rigid, they were counted on by others precisely because they were predictable. Their dedication to their work was unquestioned. After a time, both men started to change. That is when we listened to the one man speak about himself and when we heard the second man's colleagues speak about him. Both men moved away from being punctual and steady workers. Did they move from fixation?

While both men appear to have moved, they are unchanged in important ways. What remains unchanged is their addictive tendencies. What has shifted is the object of their fixatedness. At one time they were trapped in an inappropriate, project-like way of living; now one man has moved toward the excessive use of alcohol while the other has moved toward himself. Phrasing the addictions in different ways, we can say that the work-fixated man unknowingly says to himself, "I will let only the world that I can control speak to me, nothing more." The alcoholic says, "I will recognize only that world which I see after a half-dozen manhattans." Another man caught up in himself says, "I will be open to whatever and whoever give me pleasure. Someone or something that does not please me is of no interest to me."

These men, as well as what has happened to them, have been our fanciful creations, but their stories reflect our everyday efforts to deal with the difficulties of work-fixation. If we look at ourselves analytically we can say that we are always doers. At one moment we work, in another we pray, and during a third we play. As doers we bring earthy and transcendent sides of our personalities to whatever we do. With the earthy we associate warmth, flesh, and darkness; with the transcendent we are reminded of meaning, mystery, and light. When we live fixatedly as workers-at-all we have a way of pushing both the transcendent and earthy sides of ourselves so far to the background of our personalities that we live on the brittle level of isolated practicality. The price that we pay for that stance is great. Our work lacks a caring hand; our lives lack any response that moves us beyond ourselves and into the mystery of birth, death, and life.

In work-fixation we disregard both earth and heaven. It is understandable, therefore, that when we move from work-fixation we will move toward one or the other side of our forgotten selves. The man who moves toward the excessive use of alcohol is awakening to the transcendent; the man who moves toward bodily self-absorption is rediscovering the earth and his earthiness. We need to say more about this.

The man who moves toward alcoholism moves toward acknowledging the transcendent dimension of life which he had submerged under the strictures of a work-fixated approach to life. Even though the means of awakening is artificial and short-lived, the alcohol does provide an experience of freedom from overly literal behavior. During the moments after a few drinks and before too many, the alcohol induces a feeling of wholeness and well-being. Often enough we see and appreciate the beautiful after a certain amount of alcohol. Sensitivity to others is sometimes evident during these self-transcending moments. We may be grateful for the short-lived moments of transcendence that have been evidently absent for so long. The real difficulty is that the transcendence is temporary and the addiction that follows is debilitating. The use of alcohol is not a long-term solution to work-fixation, though it is frequently tried. Wanting to be kind, we say to one another that alcoholism is an occupational hazard in certain types of jobs. Perhaps, but it could also be an effort to escape from a fixated way of living that is no longer bearable.

The second man also tries to move from work-fixation. However, he does not go in the direction of the transcendent but toward the earth. His concern centers upon his bodily existence. When the body which has long been disregarded finally makes itself felt, it pulls with a vengeance. What has been denied for so long assumes an extraordinary attractiveness. The pulsing of blood and flesh can be overwhelming. In a short time we can grow astoundingly disinterested in the work that previously was our one and only concern. With the awakening of the body, the changes in our appearance and interests, resulting from our movement from work-fixation toward body-rootedness, can be as apparent as the changes that take place as we move toward alcoholism.

These changes follow an awakening of what was previously deadened. In one instance it is our earthiness; in the other, our transcendence. We can be grateful for both attempts to escape work-fixation even though these attempts become addictive. When we are alcoholic there is a desired movement toward the transcendent. When we are infatuated with our bodily being and the search for the pleasurable, we are moving toward rootedness in the earth. The difficulty is that we settle upon one side of life to the exclusion of the others, and that is likely to lead to continued difficulties.

The earthy, managing, and transcendent aspects of life are not metaphorical ways of speaking. Nor are they isolated compartments, as if we are built of three blocks which are neatly cemented together. Instead, we might think of them as representing three ever-present dimensions of life. In different situations, one or another aspect comes to the fore. They are not so distinct as to be separate; not so united as to be identical. There is a life associated with each. Ways in which we know illustrate these aspects well.

Playfully speaking, our fingers know the keyboard of a piano or typewriter better than we do. Try thinking of where to place fingers and we are sure to make a mistake. Go to the airport to meet a friend. Exchange words of welcome and greetings. Embrace. Bodies will speak and know in a way that reveals. Whether it is good to see one another will be clearly known irrespective of the words that we may utter. Our bodies know in a manner different from rational thought.

As managers we know in a manner different from an embrace. This way of knowing is also undeniable. "Two and two are four." "If you put your finger in the fire it will be burned." "I know that she will come tomorrow morning at eight o'clock." This knowledge is logical and systematic. When we become fixated as a worker this is the only kind of knowledge that we trust and recognize. Bodily ways of knowing decrease in importance. We fail to know by the embrace or by the developing ulcer. All we know is what is logical. That is why rigidity is associated with work-fixation. We are always and everywhere present as managers. It is difficult to dance as a manager; but if we are afraid of earthiness, we have to dance in that way.

There is also a transcendent element with its own way of knowing. "Let us go then, you and I, with the evening spread out against the sky . . ." (Eliot). It is difficult for the worker-at-all to know how the evening can be spread out against the sky, but poetic insight is a transcendent way of knowing that is equally as important and necessary as the more logical managing and bodily ways of knowing. However, try to live exclusively on the managing side of life and it will not be long before poetry becomes incomprehensible. So will many other realities. "Unless a man dies, he will not have life" must certainly be hocus-pocus to the fixated worker. On the other hand, if we try to live exclusively on the transcendent side of life, to the exclusion of the managing or bodily sides, we run into equally unfortunate exaggerations.

A type of closure occurs in fixation. We stay as managers. Life on the earthy and transcendent levels is beyond us. However, if we take enough drink, the transcendent opens before us. We can also consume enough alcohol to nearly obliterate bodily and managing abilities. We become unable to walk or to think systematically. We can also swing so far toward the earthy that the managing or transcendent aspects of life escape us. Even as older persons we can tend to live like infants in a peculiarly infantile manner.

Mistaken solutions to work-fixation often move fixatedly in the direction of either the earthy or the transcendent. This is understandable when as fixated workers we have long lived in a way that is heedless of earth and heaven. Shifting so whole-heartedly in one or the other direction is a relief. We discover what we have missed for so long. It is little wonder that work-fixation can easily lead to alcoholism on the one hand or a Bohemian way of living on the other. In some ways we can be grateful for the shift, for at least what has been deadened for so long is awakened.

Mistaken solutions to work-fixation indicate what is entailed in a progressive change from living fixatedly. First, movement away from fixation entails finding ways to free the transcendent and earthy aspects of ourselves so that these dimensions can be brought to whatever we do. As we move from fixation it should be less and less necessary to live mechanically. Whatever we do to help ourselves will entail becoming comfortable and gentle with the life of the earth which courses through our hearts. The movement away from work-fixation will also entail awakening to the transcendent side of ourselves. We will have to learn to become sensitive to life beyond the immediate and to linger respectfully before the incomprehensible that envelops life. For the worker-at-all, this is paradoxically frightening as well as alluring because it reflects those aspects of life that are acknowledged rather than controlled.

Second, mistaken solutions to work-fixation also warn us against substituting or stressing one side of life at the expense of another. Moving from work-fixation does not entail so accenting the transcendent that we thereby depreciate the managerial and/or bodily features of life. To try to move in that direction is to make ourselves into angels. To fixate on the earthy at the expense of the managerial and/or transcendent is to become like infants. Authentic movement from work-fixatedness entails finding ways to allow the transcendent and earthy to enter into our working hands.

Third, in addition to finding ways to facilitate the awakening of the diminished sides of life, we also have to find ways to allow our bodily and transcendent selves to come to the fore at the appropriate times. When it is time to dance we have to be able to dance. This entails the ability to leave our planning and managing selves in the background in deference to our bodily selves. When the beautiful is to be noticed or when we are inclined to rest in prayer, we have to learn to be forgetful of ourselves in order to be with worlds beyond our making. Learning to do so is not easy once we have learned to work at all of life.

And finally, our movement from work-fixation must direct us toward responsible involvement. If we cannot work as a result of efforts to move from fixation, we are doing something wrong. It is also an error to devalue work in an attempt to recover leisure.

Any long-term movement from fixedness is marked by relaxedness. Change will also be slow. Were we machines we might be able to change quickly. We are not machines even though when fixated as workers we may try to live as if we were.

We have isolated a few insights about leisure and our search for it. We know that it involves more than an effort to slow down or to safeguard a few precious moments in the midst of otherwise hectic days. Leisure is also more than a time away from the work world. What is needed is to find a gallery in the midst of life, not in the sense of a place from which to observe life but as a way to live that will facilitate involvement.

The issue surrounding work, work-fixation, and leisure is not that of being too involved. Neither is it a question of working too little. Rather, what is at issue is the base from which we are involved. Our difficulties stem from the way in which we live, that is, from what we do with and how we live in time and space. The questions that we face are: What is asked of us? What do we choose? Sensitivity and response to them are directly related to how we experience both work and leisure. Those of us caught in work-fixation are challenged in three ways: to find a way to promote awareness of what is asked of us in life, to find a spacious way to live, and to find a way to live that allows us to shift from the stance of a worker at all times to that of a worker when it is appropriate.

5 Doing Something about Work-fixation

What can we do about our difficulties? The single most important step we can take is to live deliberately enough to be tested and challenged by the question of destiny. What is asked of us in life? Are we faithful to what is asked? Those questions get to the heart of our difficulties when we speak of the riddle of work and leisure. Until we yield we will be pulled between what we want to do and what we begrudgingly have to do. As a consequence, work and leisure will remain in conflict.

The word "destiny," misused and open to distortion as it is, still conveys a truth that each of us must face. To speak of it is to awaken to "a world that loves and respects the noise and laughter of swarming children and galloping adolescents, a world that values pulsating life over mechanical things. . . . No amount of frenzied thought or logic can give us these wholesome values. . . . Man has to . . . rewin his sense of trust, his mellowness of mood, his relaxedness and belongingness. He must overcome the feeling that throws such a dismal shadow over him: that he is an accident, his life a whim, his face alien, his efforts unwanted and unneeded. The only way to do this . . . is to win back a conviction that man has a career and a destiny on this planet, a destiny which will somehow make its mark and contribute its share to the life of the whole universe."[1] Thus destiny is not something that happens to one person and not another. Neither is it reserved for only the great or

---

1. E. Becker, *Angel in Armor* (New York: Free Press – paperback, 1975), p. 152.

near-great. It is not something to be avoided or desired, unreasonable nor mystical. Destiny merely implies that the world in all its mystery has meaning.

Kierkegaard, writing to a dear friend, said this of himself: "What I really need is to become clear in my own mind *what I must do,* not what I must know—except insofar as a knowing must precede every action. The important thing is to understand what I am destined for, to perceive what the Deity wants *me* to do; the point is to find the truth which is truth *for me,* to find that idea for which I am ready to live and die. . . . It is this my soul thirsts for as the deserts of Africa thirst after water."[2] Becker, commenting on the contemporary situation, says something of the same:

> The great tragedy of our lives is that the major question of our existence is never put *by* us—it is put by personal and social impulses *for* us. Especially is this true in today's materialist, objectifying, authoritarian society, which couldn't care less about a person answering for himself the main question of his life: "What is my unique gift, my authentic talent?" As the great Carlyle saw, this is the main problem of a life, the only genuine problem, the one that should bother and preoccupy us all through the early years of our struggle for identity; all through the early years when we are tempted to solve the problem of our identity by taking the expedient that our parents, the corporation, the nation offer us; and it is the one that does bother many of us in our middle and later years when we pass everything in review to see if we really had discovered it when we thought we did. . . . The way things are set up we are rewarded, so to speak, for *not* finding our authentic talent. The result is that most of our life is in large part a rationalization of our failure to find out who we really are, what our basic strength is, what thing it is that we were meant to work upon the world. The question of what one's talent is must always be related to how he works it on the world.[3]

---

2. W. Lowrie, *A Short Life of Kierkegaard* (Princeton: Princeton University Press—paperback, 1974), pp. 82-83.

3. E. Becker, *The Birth and Death of Meaning* (New York: Free Press—paperback, 1971), p. 187.

Is our destiny in the future? Hammarskjöld says no. "Do not look back. Do not dream about the future, either. It will neither give you back the past, nor satisfy your other day-dreams. Your duty, your reward—your destiny—are here and now."[4] Destiny is an abstraction or other-worldly. What is asked has to do with our situation, talents, and responsibilities. It involves definite givens like the fact that we are married, have kids, or that we work in the inner city with poor children. It is based on the fact that we are already involved and that we find ourselves already related and in a situation that requires responsibility. The choice of what is asked is mundane and very much this-worldly. Hammarskjöld knew this as he wrote of himself in his diary: "Another opportunity was given you—as a favour and as a burden. The question is not why did it happen this way, or where is it going to lead you, or what is the price you will have to pay. It is simply *how* are you making use of it. And about that there is only *one* who can judge."[5] Newman phrased it all in a prayer:

God has created me to do Him some definite service: He has committed some work to me which He has not committed to another.

I have my mission—I may never know it in this life but I shall be told it in the next.

I am a link in a chain, a bond of connection between persons.

He has not created me for naught. I shall do His work. I shall do good.

I shall be an angel of peace, a preacher of truth in my own place while not intending it—if I do but keep His commandments.

Therefore, I will trust Him. Whatever, wherever I am I can never be thrown away.

If I am in sickness, my sickness may serve Him; if I am in sorrow, my sorrow may serve Him.

He does nothing in vain. He knows what He is about.

---

4. D. Hammarskjöld, *Markings* (London: Faber and Faber—paperback, 1964), p. 134.

5. Ibid., p. 135.

He may take away my friends. He may throw me among strangers.
    He may make me feel desolate, make my spirits sink, hide my
    future from me —
still He knows what He is about.

Besides living deliberately before the question of what is asked of
us, we can help ourselves move from work fixation by doing something
as commonplace, yet profound, as becoming attentive to how we use
words, space, and time. That effort can move us toward the world of
responsible involvement which brings with it the rediscovery of leisure.
Attentiveness to these realities is both more difficult and surprisingly
more helpful than is immediately evident.

Becoming Attentive to Our Words

Words form us as we form them. Think of the way in which we
use the word "work." We work ourselves into rages. We work at becoming just. We also work a piece of silver into a bracelet. A pump is worked
by hand and we also work off a debt. We can work it so that someone
can take a vacation. We can also work the management into giving us
free tickets. Hinges work better when oiled. Some woods work much
more easily than others. We work a zipper loose. Last night we worked
on their sympathies. Joe can work himself into or out of almost any situation. If we speak of working on another's sympathies in the same way
that we speak of working on a piece of metal, it will not be long before
both actions resemble one another. Why? Because words change us.
    Words are important. An aggressive man seeking for the tender word
moves in the direction for which he yearns. An embittered woman
recognizes her words are harsh, tempers them, and thus moves ever so
slowly toward a new-found care. In this way words are sacred. They
are one way in which the world is being created. They are also pro-
phetic in that they announce what will be. That is why one of the most
important ways to move from fixation is to be attentive to the words
we use. The effort to be attentive profoundly influences the way in which
we live.

Consider how our words shape one another. Two persons meet:

—Are you busy?
—Yes. Always. You wouldn't believe how much I have to do. I have to . . .

We pose the question "Are you busy?" to one another often. When we are caught in work-fixation, our usual response is to tell the other how busy we are. Suppose that we changed the way we answered:

—Are you busy?
—No, not too busy.

At first such a way of answering may sound like a lie, for the fact is that we do feel the pressure of what still remains unfinished. But there is always unfinished business for every person. The problem is that much of the anxiety that we feel is of our own making. That is one of the characteristics of work-fixation. Saying "No, not too busy" changes us. As soon as the words are uttered the effect can be felt. Even our conversation has to change because once we say that we are not too busy, we cannot go on speaking about all that we feel remains undone. Usually we confirm one another in our anxious ways. To say to ourselves and others that we are not particularly busy is a way of deciding not to give the turning wheel another turn to keep it moving.

Is not the question "Are you busy?" a way of politely asking another for help? If we say "no," can we not expect to be asked to do something? Consider this situation:

—Are you busy?
—No.
—Would you do this for me?
—No, I'm sorry. Not right now.
—But you're just sitting there!

Is this response selfish? Much depends on the attitude with which we speak and the way in which we say "no." Our answer can reflect a care-laden effort to life honestly. There is *always* work to be done; there are *always* people who need help. If we deny this, the only way to relax is to hide so that we cannot see what needs to be done or else to live in such a way that we cannot be found. To live hidden in this manner has the effect of perpetuating the cycle of our difficulties. Socially, we conspire with one another to remain trapped.

A "no" can hurt the feelings of the person who asks for help. It can also awaken instant anger. But the long-term effect does not hurt; neither does anger linger. We presuppose, of course, that our "no" is not given out of antipathy or anger and that there is no emergency. When it is given because we really know that a break is necessary or useful, the "no" frees us. It interrupts the rush from one thing to another in the frantic pace of the work addict. In effect, the "no" stays the rush of tasks that impinge upon us. In other words, we start living spaciously in the psychological sense explained before. The grip that the work has on us, pushing us hurriedly from one thing to another, is broken. We have time to honestly face what we have to do. We become involved, as distinguished from being busy. We have a chance to choose and to control the task rather than have the task dominate us.

Such a "no" may evoke guilt feelings, partly because we are no longer rushing along as before and partly because we may feel that we fail the other person who asks for help. But this is not authentic guilt. Instead it is a feeling of uncomfortableness that arises because we have deviated from a (harmful) routine to which we have been addicted.

Even though we may feel uncomfortable saying "no," the long-term effect is a liberating one. When we are peacefully and quietly able to maintain this stance of freedom, it will grow easier. The "no" may also become liberating for others to whom it is addressed. Of course, initially they may be angry but we will likely be able to lead them to understand that our refusal is not an expression of unfriendliness. If they do understand, they will know that we, on our part, will not impose upon them when they need the occasion to distance themselves from the busyness of overcommitment. With this kind of honesty we can live comfortably together. We create a space for one another to live other than as workers. This is the kind of space to which we referred when we spoke of leisure and the need to find a spacious way to live.

When words create a space in which it is acceptable to be other than workers, we are freed to respond generously to the requests of others. A choice can be made regarding the ways in which to be involved. There is space to be generous. Without such space, involvement stems from compulsion and assistance is offered with resentment.

There is risk involved in mentioning examples of specific behavior to illustrate the attitudes to which we have referred. What is fitting action for one person is not always informed activity for another. Nevertheless, we can suggest that, whenever we notice another person living in a way in which we wish to live, it is important to express our appreciation verbally. Words are important not only for those who hear them but for those who speak, as well.

Someone is reading and we cannot:
"It is good to see you reading."

Someone is peacefully involved and we are anxious:
"You seem so peaceful."

Someone is relaxing and we have a deadline to meet:
"How good it is to see you relaxing."

All of this is not easy. Often our words will freeze on our lips as we feel hypocritical in face of knowing that we are upset at those who seem so relaxed or unresponsive to life about them. It is difficult to become gracious when we live in a fixated way as workers. What seems like a simple statement—that we need to become attentive to our words—becomes difficult because it touches the core of our being. The more attentive we become to our speech patterns, the more we begin to recognize what underlies our need to work always and at everything.

Becoming Attentive to the Place in Which We Live

If words change us, so does the place in which we live. A second thing that we can do for ourselves is to become attentive to how it changes us. Space speaks, though without words and almost always below the surface of immediate awareness. That is why space influences us so greatly. We are hardly aware of the way in which it forms us. Have we not entered a stranger's home and even before meeting the family felt either welcome or unwelcome? The way that places are decorated tell us to be careful, relaxed, proper, or stiff without a word being spoken. No sign is needed.

Where we live can shape us as workers. Suppose, figuratively speaking, that we live above the store. Suppose, too, that space tells us that it is acceptable to work, sleep, eat, and flop exhausted before a television. Suppose that there is no space to play, to rest, or to speak comfortably with others. Suppose that there are no reminders of love, no roses, and little to refresh one's spirit but only reminders to return to work. Such space shapes us. If work-fixation is a difficulty for us, we need to be attentive to our use of the space in which we live.

Attentiveness to the space in which we work, as when we have a job, is important; but often we do not have control over this area. All of us, however, have some control over the space in which we live apart from work. For some this space is a home; for others it is an apartment. Even the monk has a room. Rich or poor, we have the opportunity to arrange the space in which we live. The space need not be large. The arrangement does not have to be costly; it can always be beautiful. Suppose that we have nothing more than a room to call our own. Let us first think about the significance of this space and then ask some questions.

Rooms are places where we express ourselves. We fix our rooms as we like. "This is my room," we say. Others hardly need to be told because there is a genuine harmony between ourselves and our rooms. Others can guess which room is ours. We leave a stamp on the world that we handle.

We can sense the relationship between our room and ourselves when we go into another's room when he or she is not there. We even feel the difference. We know that we are walking in a space that belongs to another in a personal way. We do not search through the other person's desk, closet, or bureau. If we do, there is an uncomfortableness about it. We know that we are dealing with another's private life in which we have no right to trespass. Because our rooms are so personal we feel that we can be ourselves in them. The public person can be left at the door. Sometimes when we close the door we utter a sigh of relief! The world is, as it were, left behind us. We even do things in the privacy of our rooms that we would not do in public. It is okay to be sloppy. Many a room knows a tear-stained pillow. In our room there is no need for a facade. We can be ourselves.

Rooms have a language all their own. Each room speaks. They reflect how our interiority has developed. Some rooms speak of work; others of sleep. A bedroom is very different from a room in which there is a bed. Our rooms call us to something and it is helpful to consider their message.

Some questions: What does the space in which we live say? Does it tell us to hurry? Remind us of what remains unfinished? Does its clutter reflect our inability to concentrate and the scattered directions of our activities? Is its coldness an indication of what has happened to us? Is the space our own or do we merely inhabit it? Mindful of the museum, its space, and its effect on both consciousness and involvement, what happens to us as we go to our rooms? What is the feeling that comes over us when we close the door behind us?

Similar to the way in which words keep us living in a worklike way, and similar to the manner in which a "no" can break that circle, attentiveness to the space in which we live has the effect of breaking a circle or of creating space which allows us to live other than as a worker. For instance, one difficulty in work-fixation is that we cannot leave work—in the sense of a job—behind at any time. The job becomes the arena in which we live with less conflict. The way in which we live *all the time* is acceptable and encouraged when there is a job to be done. Consequently, we spend a lot of time on the job simply because it is more comfortable for us. Yet if we want to move away from living fixatedly, we have to leave our job behind at some point in the day. A briefcase which is brought home and placed in the living room does not help us. Neither does a pile of uncorrected test papers left on the top of the desk in our bedroom. Using space in this way, the last thing we see at night and the first thing to be seen in the morning is unfinished work. Combine this reminder with the psychic drain that we already carry as a result of fixation and we have another example of a closed circle that traps us as workers-at-all.

Becoming Attentive to the Use of Time

Leisure is not merely time apart from work. Work-fixation is something more than spending long hours at a job. Even though finding leisure and avoiding fixation involve more than safeguarding moments apart from work, moving from a fixated way of living involves special attentiveness to the use of time. This is because once we live fixatedly as workers, most minutes of every day are lived in the same way. We experience no change between one minute and the next. There is only the extended moment of work called by many different names.

Surprisingly, a certain rigidity is needed to move from work-fixation. A somewhat rigid schedule can free us from the rigidity of fixation. This is true because in fixation there is no rhythm of life at all. That is why we have to discipline ourselves to some extent if we want to escape fixation. We have to plan our use of time.

The need to plan life in any way is particularly difficult once we awaken to the fact that we have been living fixatedly and once we realize what that way of living has done to us. In a short time we learn to distrust organization on any level; we run from anything that resembles discipline. We associate planning, schedules, and discipline with the things that got us into trouble in the first place. Yet, fearful or not, it is attentiveness to the use of time and a consequent planning of it that helps free us from fixation.

How we use time reflects what we value. To catch a glimpse of those values we can look back on a day that has passed and evaluate ourselves. It can be done by drawing a twenty-four hour clock.

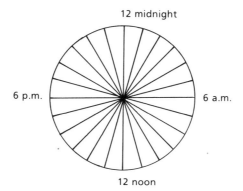

Then, after choosing a day that is recent enough to remember easily, we reconstruct how we spent the moments of that particular day.
The clock may look like this:

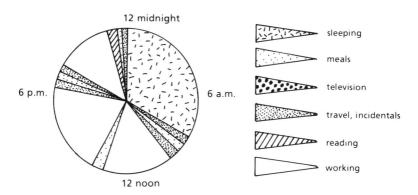

If we distrust what is revealed by looking at a single day, then we can draw other clocks representing other days. What we see is a visual portrayal of how we use time. As crude as the image can be for those of us who live fixatedly, we see the reflection of what we value. Are we comfortable with what we see? Are the hours that we spend at work too few? too many? Do our Saturdays and Sundays resemble weekdays? Do we have time for those activities that we need simply to maintain health? Is there sufficient time for sleep, relaxation, quiet, physical exercise, and eating? Do any of our activities force us to change our project-like stance as workers, or do we avoid such situations by having time for friends, family, husband, or wife? If we do have time to eat, do we ever have time to dine? These are the questions that we can ask ourselves.

If we do live fixatedly, and if we do want to change, we can plan the future in a way that will make us aware of areas of life that we tend to disregard. By setting aside time we help ourselves to be other than worker.

After looking at the past, machine-like though it appears, we can draw a twelve-month calendar that takes us into the future. It is important to see the entire year laid out before us. On the calendar we chart a rhythm of life which includes activities that seem to escape unless planned. We may choose to take time for recreative activities, professional stimulation, spiritual refreshment, vacations with family and friends, exercise, work, or any other activities which constitute a special difficulty for us.

The importance of planning is related to the fact that in work-fixation we lose perspective in the midst of everyday life. We become overwhelmed by the force of the present moment and by the demands made upon us. Spontaneity, which leads others to a balanced life, leads us in only one direction—work. Consequently, when we become work-fixated we have to start to follow somewhat blindly decisions that we made about ourselves in more balanced moments. The plan we speak of is not one that constricts but one that makes the most of organizational abilities which allow time for worlds beyond the work-like.

This is unreasonable. Who lives that way? Who can schedule life in this way? Who wants to? There are meetings to attend and things to do that can never be foreseen. How can I tell when my kids are going to get sick? Who can predict my office work? I don't live in this world alone! It's crazy to try to live by that kind of planning.

We are not speaking of everyone's need to live in this way. We are speaking only of those of us caught in fixation. In addition, we are referring to responsible planning that respects contingencies as well as duties. Flexible planning not only permits but also facilitates relaxing. The problem is that, if we do not take a responsible stance in the planning of our lives, they will be structured for us by the demands of others and the institutions for which we work. We can choose to live in such a way that others determine how we are going to spend every moment of each day, but we must also live with the consequences. It will not be long before we have the feeling that others are living our lives for us. We will also have to live with our understandably angry feelings toward those who make demands upon us.

This all sounds too self-centered. What we need is to forget about ourselves and get down to work. There is too much self-pity around, too much introspection.

We can all become self-centered and overly individualistic. That is unfair to ourselves and to those with whom we live and work. However, to think that we are so endowed as individuals that everything we have to offer is of value is equally self-centered and haughty. Today we are likely to err on the side of downplaying our inward needs rather than of basking in self-centeredness.

Planning life in this way sounds like work-fixation all over again. It's the same thing as living by the clock.

There is a difference. The planning of the future as we speak of it and the life planning that resembles living fixatedly by the clock differ in attitude and practice. To form some concept of the difference, imagine a dense crowd in the midst of which we try to push others aside in an effort to breathe more freely. We do not add anything to our lives at such times so much as we provide space for ourselves. The same is true of our planning when we strive to move from fixation. We do not add things to our days so much as we provide an opening for the life that lies under the crust of fixation. An arbitrary example illustrates the difference.

> **Plan:** I want to set aside fifteen minutes each day, early in the morning, to do nothing.

That decision seems easy enough for someone so inclined. It is also the kind of planning that can facilitate a movement away from work-fixation. Let us try to trace how such planning can help.

First, a word of clarification. We can never do "nothing." We are always doing something if we are alive. Consequently it may seem more helpful to speak of a time for "quiet" rather than a time to do "nothing." However, for reasons that will become evident, we will continue to refer to "fifteen minutes to do nothing."

To take fifteen minutes each day, early in the morning, to do nothing is almost impossible for the work-fixated person. The resolution just seems pointless. Why sit and do nothing for fifteen minutes? Anybody can do that. The fact is that the worker-at-all cannot, even though it seems easy to do.

> —I heard that you've been trying to "do nothing" for fifteen minutes each morning. What's it like?
>
> —No problem at all. It seems useless to me but I'm doing it for the hell of it.

> —How's that quiet coming?
>
> —I'm still doing it most of the time—maybe four days a week. Still nothing's happening!
>
> —What did you do this morning?
>
> —Nothing; just sat there. I did hear my favorite song on the radio and I really enjoyed it.
>
> —Tomorrow, why not leave the radio off?

— Still doing that fifteen minutes of nothing?

— Most of the time.

— Do anything special this morning?

— No. Oh, yes I did. I remember that I thought for a time about giving up cigarettes. The one I was smoking left a lousy taste in my mouth, and I thought I might as well try to stop smoking as long as I'm on this kick of trying to live a more balanced life.

— Tomorrow, why not forget about smoking during those fifteen minutes?

— You won't believe this, but do you know what I realized this morning? That for the past four weeks I've clipped my nails every morning during those few minutes!

It is difficult to sit and to do nothing for fifteen minutes. We have to try it for a time to realize how difficult it is. We speak of doing nothing in the sense of having a time to sit quietly with ourselves during which we stop reaching for books, lighting cigarettes, turning on the radio or television, sipping coffee, or clipping nails. We do not speak of the time as one that involves an effort to empty our minds of all thoughts. Instead we are envisioning a less complicated activity — merely sitting with ourselves with no particular project in mind. We might day-dream. We might muse about the way in which we live. Our thoughts may turn to others. Maybe we will become mindful of the long workday that lies ahead. What we do not want to do is get up from our chair to start that day of activity. We want to learn to sit quietly; that is not so easy.

It is helpful to take those fifteen minutes early in the morning and before the rush of the day's activities begins. When we wake from sleep there is usually a settled though tenuous togetherness about ourselves notwithstanding a surface grogginess and the trance-like quality of our consciousness. Sometimes we rise agitated, but more frequently a night of sleep brings a quietness of its own. As body-persons the chemistry of our lives continues during sleep. As spirit-persons another life is lived without our conscious awareness. We can go to bed feeling troubled but awake refreshed. We can retire apparently at peace yet awake unsettled.

Sleep, even in times of agitated rest, usually tends toward quieting and integration. Rest works toward giving us back to ourselves, but we must learn how this occurs. We have an inkling of the restorative power of sleep when we realize how we scurry to bed when the world becomes overpowering, when we have a splitting headache, and when we want to get away from it all. Awaking in the morning or after a nap, we often discover that distance has given us a new perspective.

The quieting that we find as a result of sleep is easily lost. Agitation can take hold of us so swiftly and totally that by the time we have finished washing we are already beside ourselves. As our thoughts turn restlessly to the hours ahead, we sense that the forthcoming activities of the day are predetermining our lives for us. We become agitated either with anticipation or dread. We feel tired even before the workaday world begins and in spite of the fact that we have had sufficient rest by the clock.

As mentioned earlier, the effort to set time aside to do nothing may seem pointless at first; however, it is not long before we begin to recognize the calmness that inaction facilitates. How difficult it is to sit with our own silence! But if we continue this discipline of sitting we may also find some surprisingly good reasons to persevere.

One person:

I love those fifteen minutes. I wouldn't stop them for anything. When I sit there I think of all the things that I have to do during the day and then jot them down. Then I arrange them in order of importance and tack them up on the kitchen door. What a great help it is. I'm more realistic about what I can do during the day and at night I've a sense of accomplishment.

Another person:

The reason that I like those minutes is that my imagination is more alive in the morning. That helps me with my poetry. What I do is write down in chuck-like fashion the images that come up at the time. During the day I work them out. I'm publishing more these days and I feel more alive.

The apparent rewards of taking time for quiet early in the morning are real stumbling blocks for those of us who are work-fixated. Discovering how helpful the discipline of quiet is, we are tempted to latch on to the discipline because it is so productive. We could help ourselves more by letting go of its usefulness. For instance, if we do have the good fortune to remember what has to be done during the day or if we do seem particularly creative during the fifteen minutes, it is better to refrain from writing down our lists and images. That only turns the time back into work and we remain caught in our fixated ways. Then even quiet time ends up serving our need to work always and everywhere. The way we use the time for quiet is meant to create a space for a few minutes apart from work. To turn the time back into work may help to enliven a world that has been deadened by fixation, but it will not help us to move away from living fixatedly. The problem is that in work-fixation we live so removed from ourselves and so isolated from what we may call our inwardness, that we fear a failure to jot down some thought will result in its being lost to us forever.

It takes a long time to learn to trust ourselves enough to let go of a fleeting thought or image to discover worlds that would otherwise go unnoticed because of the way we live. What work-fixated person realizes that an insight of early morning quiet could recur in the midst of a busy day? The temptation is to discover the value of quiet and then turn it back into work.

We have spoken of changing from living fixatedly to attention to time, space, and our use of words. We have spoken glibly; to actually shift the way that we live is difficult. Change is seldom easy, especially on the level we have been considering. Think of how difficult it is on the level of behavior. Tennis is illustrative. To improve we have to learn to serve effectively. That involves learning new ways of doing things. Someone has to show us the techniques. Even at that, we are apt to disregard his or her suggestions in favor of familiar and more comfortable ways of serving. At first, these suggested methods may not work so well as our old ways. However, if we resist, we never improve our game. We have to surrender in order to learn. If this is true on the level of behavior, it is even more keenly felt in matters that touch the life of the heart—values, hopes, dreams, memories, and loves.

The closer to the heart that we are challenged, the more resistance we find. And that is as it should be. We have to protect ourselves in this way, for we know intuitively how valuable we are. However, if we are going to move from work-fixated ways, we have to overcome the resistance to change within ourselves. There is a surrender involved. Fortunately, attention to the way we use words, time, and space involves only a surrender to ourselves. We do not have to rely on gurus, special potions, or exotic remedies. It is not a call to surrender responsibility for ourselves. Rather, we are left to face our own integrity. We have no one to delude but ourselves. And this, also, is as it should be.

6 Creativity, Spirituality, and the Religious Person

Breaking away from work-fixation awakens our own lives as well as the world about us. We rediscover what is so easily forgotten—namely, our value as persons who work. Valuable though the diverse works we do may be, much depends on how we are present while we do them. What goes into the making of a nurse's hands or our own is of significance. What we bring to our work makes a difference. If we forget or are unable to be attentive to life apart from work, not only is our work less than it could be, but the valuableness of our presence escapes as well. Our past, our present, and our dreams—the constellation of values that we embody—find their way into our hands whether we understand the image of hands in a literal or figurative sense.

We are an ever-shifting and continually developing body of possibilities. At one moment we are persons at play, at another we are at work. When we are with some people, we act one way; with others, we behave differently. In every situation and to each different activity we bring another face, yet through each change we remain the same person. In many ways we resemble kaleidoscopes. They are the same glass beads through which we see light, but with every turn of the cylinder we see a new world before us because of the way the beads arrange themselves.

Another image that captures something of our experience of human presence is a drawing like the following:

When we look at it in one way we see a vase. However, if we continue to look at the drawing, we can see two persons looking at one another. Once both images are recognized, we can then shift back and forth between them. When we analyze what happens, it is easy to see that we perceive in differing ways, depending upon which color forms the background of the picture. When white is to the foreground, we see one image; when black shifts from background to foreground, we see the second.

What do these ways of understanding our varieties of presence suggest? For one thing, they explain how one worker's hand differs from another's. If we want to work as nurses, there is a technical proficiency that we have to bring to what we do: how to bandage wounds, give injections, and roll patients in order to make their beds. That technical ability forms the foreground of our presence. With it we can get a job done. But what forms the background of our presence is also vitally important. What accompanies our technical proficiency holds a key to understanding how valuable our presence is. In great part that background presence is the difference between a machine-like presence and one that is deeply human.

Understanding human presence in this way also illustrates why it is so necessary to be other than worker, sometimes. Times apart from it influence the way our hands are at work. There has to be a time, if our hands are to be made tender, when compassion comes to the fore rather than stays in the background. That is why attention to words, time, and place are so necessary to free us from fixation. They provide a space to breathe, a chance to be present in another way. What happens to us in those moments finds its way back into our hands.

From what we have said we can understand that it is worth asking ourselves: What do we make room for in our lives? Phrased another way: How do we use time and space? Without an explicit time for play, it is not likely that we will be playful in the midst of involvement. Without a determinate period for reflection, it is unlikely that we will be reflective in the midst of activity.

Here one of the misfortunes of work-fixation becomes evident. Life apart from work remains beyond appreciation and its real worth cannot be seen when we stand only as workers. The stance of the worker readies us only for certain things. Two and two make sense if we are workers. Poetry does not. Neither can the language of our bodies be understood when we stand only as workers. Most tellingly, our value as persons escapes appreciation and awareness. The values that we do find are those that make sense in terms of work. The worker-at-all can only understand his or her value in terms of work. This is understandable since it is only this aspect of his or her presence that remains to the fore of personality.

Does the effort to overcome work-fixation suggest that we have to downplay the importance of work? No. Quite the contrary. On one hand our lives as workers are refreshed and on the other our work becomes creative. Why? Because attention to words, space, and time has the effect of disentangling us from our busyness. A distance is created between ourselves and our task. That space favors flexibility, the ground out of which creativity emerges. To see this clearly, it would help to speak of work-fixation as a difficulty of over-identification.

When fixated, we over-identify with what we do. We become fused with our work. For reasons unknown to us, we begin to equate our lives with what we do. The two poles of life, ourselves and the world, merge into one. Not that they are ever separable; they are, however, distinguishable experientially. Over-identification makes it difficult to envision our lives as distinct in any way from what we do as workers. If our work is criticized, we are criticized; if our work is judged to be "good," then we are "good." There develops an equation rather than a relation between our lives and what we do. We are not saying that we ever remain aloof or unaffected by our work and the reception it receives. What we are saying is that in over-identification we become affected in an exaggerated and unhealthy way. We become too easily tense, nervous, and agitated. As a result our work also suffers.

If we become over-identified, work is used almost solely to build ourselves. In the process we forget that the world we fashion has a life and value of its own. We demand that persons become successful students in order to show that we are successful teachers. We drive our company into prominence because that enhances our own worth. Once we discover a formula for success in whatever task we are about, we use that same formula over and over again for fear that another may be less successful. Hence, the artist repeatedly paints without fresh insight or spontaneity; the teacher teaches in the same way; the author writes a novel that hardly differs from a previous one. Our lives begin to acquire a sameness and predictability that stifle creativity. That is why it is so necessary to allow a liberating space between ourselves and our work when we are trapped in work-fixation.

When we allow enough distance to develop, work can have a life of its own. Work is freed. Who has not had the experience of being surprised by what they have made? In the midst of sculpturing we follow the wood and a chance chip leads in an unexpected direction. In an effort to prepare a meal we season appropriately as the need arises and the flavor develops. The ability to experiment and to change in the midst of the preparation distinguishes the creative cook from the person who warms food. How many of us in the process of speaking, teaching, or writing have not discovered that our insights and understanding were far more extensive than we realized before we began to speak, teach, or write? In each instance we have to be able to allow work a life of its own if our activity is to be creative. We cannot do this when fixated. Hence creativity is absent. To be creative, we have to let the work form us as we form it. Then the circle of creativity is enlivening.

There is a reward involved in allowing such creativity. First, it may be surprising how our projects can take us where we did not plan to go. In work-fixation, that element is missing because everything is figured out ahead of time. All we have to do is carry out our plans slavishly. When we are prepared to look at what we form, when we allow a space between our projects and ourselves, we are open to surprise. The student, the insight, the hospital staff, or the wood with which we work all share in the mystery of life. Allowing for the possibility of newness relieves some of the dullness which necessarily accompanies all work. With a little distance we can contemplate and be enlivened by what we make.

The creativity to which we refer is not to be equated with inventions, pioneering thought, or revolutionary undertakings. That kind of creativity—call it cultural creativity—is the gift of relatively few. All of us, however, have the gift of personal creativity, whereby work is creative insofar as it changes and inspires us as we fashion the future.

Second, permitting an appropriate distance between ourselves and our work is freeing. From ever so slight a distance we can get new perspectives on success and failure, praise and blame. Not only do we become more flexible as a result, but we can also become more playful. We relinquish some of the seriousness about work that is too ponderous and confining to be helpful.

Last, a suitable distance enables us to respond better as needs arise. When we are fixated, what looks like concern for the work at hand is concern for ourselves. Work is used obliquely for a purpose apart from itself. Once an appropriate space develops between ourselves and our work, unappreciated jobs, work that goes unnoticed, tasks above or beneath our sense of dignity can all be undertaken out of a sensitivity to what is to be done. We can let our images (exalted or humble) and the results (success or failure) play a secondary role in the entire process of why and how we are involved. And we will be surprised how much the ability to be attentive to our work develops.

It is unfortunate when we fall into work-fixation. In the process we lose a sense of personal value as well as the value of our work. An added misfortune is the loss of creativity. What is even more unfortunate is that religion as a living reality is eclipsed, and in the resulting obscurity life is robbed of its ultimate context. Today, given the widespread nature of work-fixation, it is the religious worker who is so desperately needed.

We use the word "religious" hesitantly since it is so often a source of division among us. The religious worker, for one, lives with an awareness that life—which is so tenuously strung between birth and death—is a gift and embedded in mystery. The work approach to every aspect of living closes us to that realization and consequently to the world of lived-religion. Lived-religion encompasses work, play, prayer, and every other activity in a harmonious unity. This way of living was exemplified by Pope John XXIII.

John seemed to be at peace. When we read his letters and journal and when we recall him in situations ranging from state functions to dining with an artist friend, visiting a jail or speaking to midwives, we discover that in all of these situations he appeared at ease. To be that way he must have been at home in the world. Evidently he could let things be as he found them. The projects that he did have must have been grounded somewhere other than in his own isolated intention for the world.

He frequently said that he lived in God's world, and to the observer it would seem as though this was more than a passing awareness. He spoke of being a guest on the earth. We live differently in a home as guests than when it is our own. We also use things differently. When we borrow another's car, there is a way in which the owner accompanies us. His presence may not be entirely conscious, but it is nonetheless real. We drive accordingly. If we are angry with him, we may drive a little more aggressively. Ordinarily, though, we are more caring with another's property. This must be something of how John lived in God's world. He carried God with him, if not consciously, nonetheless in a genuine manner.

As a guest in God's world, John seemed to feel at home and could live graciously and respectfully. If he were relaxed in a variety of situations it was probably because he realized that the world was not totally his. This is a different experience from feeling either totally responsible for or totally alienated from life.

If our analogy of living in God's world and another's house is accurate, then it is understandable how a religious person might be so relaxed. In God's world, as in another's house when we are welcome there, everything is to be used as if it were our own. Our hosts want us to feel that way. When we are guests we are receivers of a gift. Nothing is ours, yet everything is ours. Demands are in the background. They seemed to be in the background in John's life.

His way of living also seems to tell us how precious a gift life is. Letting that realization influence us would lighten every moment. When something is a valuable gift we are gentle with it. We handle it carefully. More often than not it is surprising. We can tell when another cherishes our gift when we watch him hold it. When we look at John we can say that he saw the world as a gift, for he held it that way. He must have realized the gift of his own life as well, for he was also gentle with himself.

John was a person who called himself religious. Some who live religiously, as we have used the word, may not refer to themselves as such. However, to distinguish who is and who is not religious is not our intention. Instead we want to indicate that *lived* religious presence is characterized by certain attitudes, qualities, and abilities, among which are receptivity, surrender (not passivity), compassion, respect, care, openness, a sense of mystery, and an ability to stand contemplatively before the inexpressible. We are not saying that the sum of these attitudes and abilities constitutes religious presence. We are saying that a person who lives religiously has these abilities and attitudes.

The woman whose touch as a nurse was unforgettable portrays religious presence. Let us call her an image of a religious person as a worker. A host of values, attitudes, realizations, and experiences were expressed in the way she worked. She had the same technical ability as any nurse, but it was her presence, what she brought to her work as a person, that was so important.

Consider the fixated worker. When an aggressive stance of work is not tempered by a compassionate stance, one dominates the other. The unchecked aggressive stance leads to a war-like presence. When a critical stance is not tempered by an accepting one, we are led to live against and apart from others. Such a way of living ends in alienation unless it yields at times to an appreciative, restful dwelling with others. When a manipulative stance is not tempered by a receptive one, we become dictators. Considered from this angle, the religious person as worker is a shepherd of human values. In an authentic way, the religious person stands uniquely at the center of culture. Such a person embodies, preserves, and furthers fully human living. But this is possible only when one brings a *lived* religious presence to life and not simply a set of practices or a system of beliefs unrelated to daily life.

One problem with speaking of the religious person as standing uniquely at the center of culture is that we live in one that is work-fixated. As a result, religion is unthinkingly associated with other-worldly concerns or reduced to special projects ranging from saying prayers to specialized social involvement. In such a situation the sacredness of life and of the world about us escape our experience. We designate special kinds of work as holy. Priests and ministers do holy work. So do others who are occupied with activities associated with church life. In a society where work-fixation is widespread, to work as a bank-teller, mathematician or stenographer is secular. When we speak of a religious person standing at the center of culture we run the risk of associating such a person with a particular profession rather than with a sense of presence. We can avoid some misconceptions and distortions resulting from such an image when we realize that everyone is destined, as human, to stand at the center of culture. When does this occur? When we bring a caring presence to whatever we do. What will be its sign? That we are no longer surprised at being able to stand contemplatively before the deeper values of life with respect, openness, and a sense of mystery.

In a way it is tragic when the lived religious dimension of life becomes deadened. It is a tragedy because the religious aspect of existence is integral to life. Without it service tends to become fanatical, cold, and dehumanized. At the same time we turn our back on what could be potentially our unique and indispensable contribution to others.

Each person, as religious, stands at the center of culture. Each embodies, preserves, and furthers the human. What we do with space and time, how we live, the words we use, are of the utmost importance. Our uniqueness lies in the way that we live before God and others. Religious persons are at home in any employment. Everything is sacred. All life, each thing, every happening, holds the potential recognition of its sacredness.

The lived awareness of the presence of God in life is a gift, one given to all. We can destroy that gift by the way we live. We can deaden or enliven ourselves and the world about us by the way we live. In a profound way we are responsible for ourselves. Only we can live our lives and die our deaths. No one can do either for us. To the extent we forfeit that responsibility, we relinquish being human.

Bibliography

For Reading

LITERATURE

Potok, C. *My Name Is Asher Lev.* New York: Fawcett (paperback), 1972.
Delightful reading. A novel describing a man's slow and painful discovery of his unique life work (his "ought"). The book is helpful because it powerfully portrays the cost and dignity of being faithful to one's calling (what is asked) in life.

MEDICINE

Friedman, M., and Rosenman, R. *Type A Behavior and Your Heart.* Greenwich, Conn.: Fawcett (paperback), 1974.
Racy, popularized, and challenging. The book is important insofar as it describes the clearly defined pattern of life that we have called "work-fixation" and that the authors term "Type A behavior."

PSYCHIATRY

Frankl, V. *The Doctor and the Soul.* New York: Bantam (paperback), 1965.
Of special importance is the chapter entitled "The Meaning of Work." It can be read without reading the entire book. The chapter is especially significant because of its underlying thought: "Work does not of itself make a person indispensable and irreplaceable; it only gives a person a chance to be so."

PSYCHOLOGY

Kilpatrick, William. *Identity and Intimacy.* New York: Delta (paperback), 1975.

Identity and intimacy are directly related to work-fixation. This text—well-written, critical, informed, and interesting—does not directly relate identity to work and work-fixation, but the relationship is evident as the text is read.

SPIRITUALITY

Lindbergh, A. *Gift from the Sea.* New York: Vintage (paperback), 1965.

A text written from the perspective of a woman distanced from her everyday involvement as mother, wife, and professional person. The examples she uses and the tone of the writing clearly speak of leisure as a spacious way of living.

Van Kaam, Adrian. *On Being Involved.* Denville, N.J.: Dimension (paperback), 1970.

Concise and meditative. Within the short text the natural rhythm between involvement and detachment is explained in a refreshing and helpful manner.

THEOLOGY

Keen, S. *Apology for Wonder.* New York: Harper and Row, 1969.

Chapter 5, "The Travail of Homo Faber," is an interesting presentation built around the theme: when one becomes primarily a worker-at-all, wonder, as well as many other dimensions of life, disappear. The author traces how this distortion may happen and then develops an image of human beings much broader than that of workers.

See also:

CONCERNING THE SIGNIFICANCE OF WORDS

Gusdorf, Georges. *Speaking.* Translated by Paul T. Brockelman. Evanston: Northwestern University Press, 1965.

Picard, Max. *The World of Silence.* Translated by Stanley Godman. Chicago: Henry Regnery, 1964.

CONCERNING THE USE OF SPACE

Harbison, Robert. *Eccentric Spaces.* New York: Alfred A. Knopf, 1977.

CONCERNING THE USE OF TIME

Mackenzie, R. Alec. *The Time Trap.* New York: AMACOM, 1972. (From the perspective of management). Along the same lines, refer to Alan Lakein's paperback, *How to Get Control of Your Time and Your Life.*

CONCERNING "WHAT IS ASKED" OF US IN LIFE

Becker, Ernest. *The Birth and Death of Meaning.* New York: Free Press, 1971. (See especially pp. 186ff.)

Dunne, John S. *The Reasons of the Heart.* New York: Macmillan, 1978. (See especially pp. 18ff.)

Kierkegaard, Søren. *Purity of Heart.* Translated by Douglas V. Steere. New York: Harper and Row (Torchbooks), 1956. (See especially pp. 197ff.)

Maslow, Abraham. *Eupsychian Management.* Homewood, Ill.: Dorsey Press, 1965.

——. *The Farther Reaches of Human Nature.* New York: Penguin, 1976. (See especially pp. 106ff.)

For Study

ACCOUNTS OF EVERYDAY WORK EXPERIENCES

Frazer, Ronald. *Work: Twenty Personal Accounts.* 2 vols. New York: Penguin, 1968.

Terkel, Studs. *Working.* New York: Avon (paperback), 1975.

ANTHROPOLOGY

Lee, Dorothy. *Freedom and Culture.* Englewood Cliffs, N.J.: Spectrum (paperback), 1959. Refer to chapter 3: "The Joy of Work as Participation."

Mead, Margaret. *Male and Female.* New York: Mentor (paperback), 1955. Of special importance is chapter 7: "Rhythm of Work and Play."

HISTORY

Parias, L.-H., ed. *Histoire Generale du Travail.* Paris: Nouvelle Librairie de France, 1959.

LITERATURE

Frisch, Max. *Homo Faber.* Translated by Michael Bullock. New York: Harcourt Brace Jovanovich (paperback), 1959.

Price, Reynolds. *Love and Work.* New York: Atheneum, 1975.

PHILOSOPHY

Pieper, Josef. *Leisure: The Basis of Culture.* New York: New American Library (paperback), 1963.

Simon, Yves R. *Work, Society and Culture.* Edited by Vukan Kuic. New York: Fordham University Press, 1971.

POLITICAL SCIENCE

De Grazia, Sebastian. *Of Time, Work and Leisure.* New York: Doubleday (paperback), 1964.

PSYCHOLOGY/PSYCHIATRY

Neff, Walter. *Work and Human Behavior.* New York: Atherton, 1968.

SOCIOLOGY

Ellul, Jacques. *The Technological Society.* Translated by John Wilkinson. New York: Vintage (paperback), 1967.

SPIRITUALITY

Steere, Douglas. *Work and Contemplation.* New York: Harper, 1957.

———. "Contemplation and Leisure." *Humanitas* (November 1972): 287-306.

THEOLOGY

Chenu, M. D. *The Theology of Work: An Exploration.* Translated by Lilian Soiron. Chicago: Henry Regnery, 1966.

Kaiser, Edwin G. *Theology of Work.* Ramsey, N.J.: Newman Press, 1966.

For Research

The literature on the topics of work and leisure is extensive. The following bibliography is a selected one, listing those texts directly concerned with work. References to leisure and labor, equally extensive and developed, have been omitted. Because this text has been written for those who have an opportunity to choose significant work, references from the perspective of liberation have been omitted as have those texts concerned with the specialized problems of management, automation, and adaptation to the work-place.

Anderson, Nels. *Dimensions of Work: The Sociology of a Work Culture.* New York: McKay, 1964.

————. *Work and Leisure.* New York: Free Press, 1961.

Arendt, Hannah. *The Human Condition.* Chicago: University of Chicago Press, 1958.

Aryon, Henri. *La Philosophie du Travail.* Paris: Presses Universitaires de France, 1961.

Auzias, Jean-Marie. *La Philosophie et les Techniques.* Paris: Presses Universitaires de France, 1965.

Bell, Daniel. *Work and Its Discontents.* New York: League for Industrial Democracy, 1970.

Berger, Peter, ed. *The Human Shape of Work.* New York: Macmillan, 1964.

Best, Fred. *The Future of Work.* Englewood Cliffs, N.J.: Prentice-Hall, 1973.

Biesheuvel, S. *Work and Its Effect on Personality Development in Africans.* n.p., 1963. (Holding of Duquesne University Library.)

Boissonnade, Prosper. *Life and Work in Medieval Europe.* Translated by Eileen Power. New York: Alfred Knopf, 1927.

Borne, E., and Henry, F. *A Philosophy of Work.* Translated by F. Jackson. London: Sheed and Ward, 1938.

Borow, H., ed. *Man in a World at Work.* Boston: Houghton Mifflin, 1964.

Breer, Paul, and Locke, Edward. *Task Experience as a Source of Attitudes.* Homewood, Ill.: Dorsey Press, 1965.

Brockman, Norbert. "The Workaholic Priest." *Pastoral Life* 27 (February 1978).

Bryant, Clifton, ed. *The Social Dimensions of Work.* Englewood Cliffs, N.J.: Prentice-Hall, 1972.

Buck, Vernon E. *Working Under Pressure.* New York: Crane, Russak, 1972.

Bushnell, Horace. *Work and Play.* New York: C. Scribner, 1881.

Buxton, L. H. D. *Primitive Labour.* London: Methuen, 1924.

Buytenijk, F. J. J. *Woman.* Translated by Denis J. Barrett. New York: Association Press, 1968.

Cabot, Richard Clarke. *What Men Live By: Work, Play, Love, Worship.* Boston: Houghton Mifflin, 1914.

Callahan, Sidney Cornelia. *The Working Mother.* New York: Macmillan, 1971.

Caplow, T. *The Sociology of Work.* Minneapolis: University of Minnesota Press, 1954.

Center for the Study of Liberal Education for Adults. *Meanings of Work.* Brookline, Mass., 1964.

Chardin, Teilhard de. *The Divine Milieu.* Translated by Bernard Wall. New York: Harper and Row (Torchbooks), 1965.

Chenu, M. D. *L'Évangile Dans Le Temps.* Paris: Les Éditions de Cerf, 1964.

————. *The Theology of Work: An Exploration.* Translated by Lillian Soiron. Chicago: Henry Regnery, 1966.

Childe, V. Gordon. *Man Makes Himself.* London: Watts, 1936.

Clark, Dennis. *Work and the Human Spirit.* New York: Sheed and Ward, 1967.

Colin, M. "Sociopathologie du Travail." *Cahiers de l'Institut de Science Économique Appliqueé* 21 (1965):103-113.

Cooper, Cary L., and Payne, Roy, eds. *Stress at Work.* New York: Wiley, 1978.

Crites, Joan. *Vocational Psychology.* New York: McGraw Hill, 1967.

Cull, John G. *Adjustment to Work.* Springfield, Ill.: Charles C. Thomas, 1973.

Danielsson, Bengt. *Work and Life on Roroia.* New York: Macmillan, 1955.

Delarvelle, Étienne. "Le Travail dans les Règles Monastiques Occidentales du 4ᵉ au 10ᵉ Siècle." *Journal de Psychologie Normale et Pathologique* 41 (1948):51-64.

Demva, D. "L'Idée de Travail en Occident et en Africa." *Afrique Documents* 85-86 (1966):151-157.

Dickson, Paul. *The Future of the Workplace.* New York: Weybright and Talley, 1975.

Domenach, J.-M. "Loisir et Travail." *Esprit* (1959): 1103-1110.

Draper, Jean E.; Lundgren, Earl F.; and Strother, George B. *Work Attitudes and Retirement Adjustment.* Madison: University of Wisconsin, Bureau of Business Research and Service, 1967.

Dubalen, Marie Therese. *The Worker Priests.* New York: Student League for Industrial Democracy, 1955.

Dublin, Robert, ed. *Handbook of Work, Organization and Society.* Chicago: Rand McNally, 1976.

Fichter, Joseph H. *Religion as an Occupation.* South Bend, Ind.: University of Notre Dame Press, 1961.

Fogarty, M. *The Roles of Work.* London: Chapman, 1963.

Ford, Robert N. *Motivation Through the Work Itself.* New York: Management Association, 1969.

French, David G. *Working Communally: Patterns and Possibilities.* New York: Russell Sage Foundation, 1975.

Freud, S. *Civilization and Its Discontents.* New York: W. W. Norton, 1961.

Frew, David. *The Management of Stress: Using TM at Work.* Chicago: Nelson-Hall, 1977.

Friedmann, Eugene A., and others. *The Meaning of Work and Retirement.* Chicago: University of Chicago Press, 1954.

Friedmann, Georges, and Naville, Pierre. *Traité de Sociologie de Travail.* Paris: Colin, 1962.

Fromm, Erich. *The Revolution of Hope: Toward a Humanized Technology.* New York: Harper and Row, 1968.

Ginzberg, E., and Berman, H. *The American Worker in the Twentieth Century: A History Through Autobiographies.* New York: Free Press, 1963.

Ginzberg, E., and others. *Occupational Choice: An Approach to a General Theory.* New York: Columbia University Press, 1951.

Glotz, Gustave. *Ancient Greece at Work.* New York: Barnes and Noble, 1965.

Goldstein, Bernard. *Children and Work: A Study of Socialization.* New Brunswick, N.J.: Transaction Books, 1979.

Goodman, Natalie C. *Leisure, Work and the Use of Time: A Study of Adult Styles of Time Utilization, Childhood Determinants and Vocational Implications.* Cambridge: Harvard University, 1969.

Goodwin, Leonard. *Do the Poor Want to Work? A Social-Psychological Study of Work Orientations.* Washington: Brookings Institution, 1972.

Green, Thomas F. *Work, Leisure, and the American Schools.* New York: Random House, 1968.

Gross, E. "The Worker and Society." *Man in a World at Work.* Boston: Houghton Mifflin, 1964.

Guelluy, Robert. *Le Travail dans La Vie du Chrëtien.* Gembloux: Éditions J. Dugulot, 1953.

Guitton, Jean. *Le Travail Intellectuel.* Paris: Aubier, 1951.

Hackman, Ray C. *The Motivated Working Adult.* New York: American Management Association, 1969.

Hatterer, Lawrence J. "Work Identity." *American Journal of Psychiatry* 122 (1966):1284-1286.

Hendrick, I. "Work and the Pleasure Principle." *Psychoanalytic Quarterly* 12 (1943):311-329.

Heron, Alexander R. *Why Men Work.* Stanford, Calif.: Stanford University Press, 1948.

Hersey, Rexford. *Zest for Work: Industry Rediscovers the Individual.* New York: Harper, 1955.

Herzberg, Frederick. *Work and the Nature of Man.* New York: World Publishing, 1966.

Herzberg, Frederick, and others. *Job Attitudes: A Review of Research and Opinion.* Pittsburgh: Psychological Service of Pittsburgh, 1957.

————. *The Motivation to Work.* New York: Wiley, 1959.

Holmes, D. "A Contribution to the Psychoanalytic Theory of Work." *Psychoanalytic Study of the Child* 20 (1965):384-391.

Horney, Karen. *Neurosis and Human Growth.* New York: W. W. Norton, 1950.

Howell, Barbara. *Don't Bother to Come In on Monday: What to Do When You Lose Your Job.* New York: St. Martin's Press, 1973.

Hughes, Everett C. *Men and Their Work.* Glencoe: Free Press, 1958.

Hugill, Stan. *Shanties from the Seven Seas; Shipboard Work Songs and Songs Used as Work Songs from the Great Days of Sail.* New York: Dutton, 1961.

Huizinga, Johan. *Homo Ludens: A Study of the Play Element in Culture.* New York: Beacon Press, 1955.

Jaques, Elliott. *A General Theory of Bureaucracy.* New York: Halsted Press, 1976.

————. *Work, Creativity and Social Justice.* New York: International Universities Press, 1970.

Kaufmann, Carl B. *Man Incorporate: The Individual and His Work in an Organized Society.* Garden City: Doubleday, 1967.

Kennedy, Eugene. "Stress in Ministry—An Overview." *Chicago Studies* 18 (1979):1, 5-16.

Kets de Vries, M. "Defective Adaptation to Work." *Bulletin of the Menninger Clinic* 42 (1978):35-50.

Kirn, Arthur G. *Lifework Planning.* 2 vols. Hartford: A. G. Kirn, 1974.

Kramer, Y. "Work Compulsion—A Psychoanalytic Study." *Psychoanalytic Quarterly* 46 (1977):361.

Kwant, Remy C. *Philosophy of Labor.* Pittsburgh: Duquesne University Press, 1960.

Lacroix, J. "La Notion du Travail." *La Vie Intellectuelle* (1952): 4-31.

Ladrière, Jean. "The Integration of Scientific Research with Christian Life." *Lumen Vitae* 15 (1960):433-450.

Lai, Rajendra Behari. *The Art of Working.* New York: Asia Publishing House, 1963.

Lantos, Barbara. "Metapsychological Considerations on the Concept of Work." *International Journal of Psycho-Analysis* 33 (1952):439-443.

————. "Work and the Instincts." *International Journal of Psycho-Analysis* 24 (1943):114-119.

Lehrer, Robert Nathaniel. *Work Simplification: Creative Thinking About Work Problems.* Englewood Cliffs, N.J.: Prentice-Hall, 1957.

Levenstein, Aaron. *Why People Work: Changing Incentives in a Troubled World.* New York: Crowell-Collier Press, 1962.

Levinson, D., et. al. *The Seasons of a Man's Life.* New York: Knopf, 1978.

Levinson, H. *Emotional Health in the World of Work.* New York: Harper, 1964.

Levitan, Sar A. *Work Is Here to Stay.* Salt Lake City: Olympus, 1973.

Lofquist, Lloyd H. *Adjustment to Work: A Psychological View of Man's Problems in a Work-Oriented Society.* New York: Appleton-Century-Crofts, 1969.

Longmate, Norman. *The Workhouse.* New York: St. Martin's Press, 1974.

Man, Henri de. *Joy in Work.* Translated by Eden and Cedar Paul. New York: Holt, n.d.

Maslow, Abraham. "A Theory of Metamotivation: The Biological Rooting of the Value-Life." *Humanitas* (Winter 1969): 301-343.

Mayo, Elton. *The Human Problems of an Industrial Civilization.* Boston: Division of Research, Graduate School of Business Administration, Harvard University, 1946.

McLean, A., ed. *To Work Is Human.* New York: Macmillan, 1967.

―――. *Occupational Stress.* Springfield, Ill.: Charles Thomas, 1974.

Mead, Margaret, ed. *Cultural Patterns and Technological Change.* New York: New American Library (Mentor), 1961.

Meakin, David. *Man and Work.* Cambridge: University Printing House, 1976.

Menninger Foundation. *Interdisciplinary Research on Work and Mental Health: A Point of View and a Method.* Topeka: Menninger Foundation, 1961.

Menninger, Karl. "Work as Sublimation." *Bulletin of the Menninger Clinic* 6 (1942):170-182.

Mott, Paul E. *Shift Work: The Social, Psychological and Physical Consequences.* Ann Arbor: University of Michigan Press, 1965.

Mumford, L. *The Condition of Man.* New York: Harcourt, Brace, 1944.

Myrdal, Alva, and Klein, Viola. *Women's Two Roles: Home and Work.* London: Routledge and Kegan Paul, 1967.

Neff, Walter. *Changes in the Meaning of Work During Psychiatric Rehabilitation.* Final Report, RD 1603-P. Washington, D.C.: Social and Rehabilitation Service, 1968.

Nosow, Sigmund, and Form, William. *Man, Work and Society: A Reader in the Sociology of Occupations.* New York: Basic Books, 1962.

Oates, Wayne Edward. *Confessions of a Workaholic: The Facts About Work Addiction.* n.p., 1971.

Oberndorf, C.P. "Psychopathology of Work." *Bulletin of the Menninger Clinic* 15 (1951):77-84.

Ornstein, R. *On the Experience of Time.* New York: Penguin, 1969.

Palm, Goran. *The Flight from Work.* Translated by Patrick Smith. New York: Cambridge University Press, 1977.

Parker, Stanley R. *The Future of Work and Leisure.* New York: Praeger, 1971.

Payot, Jules. *Will-Power and Work.* Translated by Richard Duffy. New York: Funk and Wagnalls, 1921.

Perrin, Henri. *Priest and Worker: The Autobiography of Henri Perrin.* Translated by Bernard Wall. New York: Holt, Rinehart and Winston, 1964.

Pieper, Joseph. *In Tune with the World: A Theory of Festivity.* Translated by Richard and Clara Winston. Chicago: Franciscan Herald Press, 1973.

Richardson, Alan. *The Biblical Doctrine of Work.* London: World Council of Churches by SCM Press, 1952.

Riedman, Sarah Regal. *The Physiology of Work and Play.* New York: Dryden, 1950.

Rodgers, Daniel T. *The Work Ethic in Industrial America.* Chicago: University of Chicago Press, 1978.

Roe, Anne. "Personality Structure and Occupational Behavior." *Man in a World at Work.* Boston: Houghton Mifflin, 1964.

Rohrlich, Jay B. *Work and Love: The Crucial Balance.* New York: Summit, 1980.

Ruskin, John. *The Crown of Wild Olive: Three Lectures on Work, Traffic and War.* New York: J. Wiley and Sons, 1887.

Ryan, John Julian. "The Semantics of Work: A Correlation of the Terms Drudgery, Toil, Labor, Work." *Humanitas* 7 (1971):133-140.

Savage, Charles M. *Work and Meaning: A Phenomenological Inquiry.* Chestnut Hill: n.p., 1973.

Schaw, Louis C. *The Bonds of Work: Work in Mind, Time and Tradition.* San Francisco: Jossey-Bass, 1968.

Schoonenburg, Peter. *God's World in the Making.* Pittsburgh: Duquesne University Press, 1964.

Scott, Donald F. *The Psychology of Work.* London: Duckworth, 1970.

Shephard, Roy J. *Human Physiological Work Capacity.* New York: Cambridge University Press, 1978.

Schutz, Alfred. *The Phenomenology of the Social World.* Translated by George Walsh and Frederick Lehert. Evanston: Northwestern University Press, 1967.

Sheehy, G. *Passages.* New York: E. P. Dutton, 1976.

Siegmeister, Elie. *Work and Sing: A Collection of the Songs That Built America.* New York: Scott, 1944.

Simmons, Ozzie G. *Work and Mental Illness: Eight Case Studies.* New York: Wiley, 1965.

Sivadon, P., and Amiel, R. *Psychopathologie du Travail.* Paris: Les Éditions Sociales Francaises, 1969.

Slocum, Walter L. *Occupational Careers: A Sociological Perspective.* 2nd ed. Chicago: Aldine, 1974.

Smith, Thomas Vernor. "Work as an Ethical Concept." *Journal of Philosophy* 21 (September 1924).

Sohn-Rethel, Alfred. *Intellectual and Manual Labour: A Critique of Epistemology.* Atlantic Heights, N.J.: Humanities Press, 1978.

Steele, Fred I. *Physical Settings and Organizational Development.* Reading, Mass.: Addison-Wesley, 1973.

Super, D. E. *The Psychology of Careers: An Introduction to Vocational Development.* New York: Harper and Row, 1957.

Susman, Gerald. *Autonomy at Work: A Sociotechnical Analysis of Participative Management.* New York: Praeger, 1976.

Tannenbaum, Frank. *A Philosophy of Labor.* New York: Knopf, 1951.

Taylor, Graham C. "Work and Leisure in the Age of Automation." *Main Currents* 22 (1966):107-115.

Theobald, Robert. "Needed: A New Definition of Work." *New University Thought* 3 (1963):9-14.

Tilgher, A. *Work: What It Has Meant to Men Through the Ages.* New York: Harcourt, Brace, 1930.

Todd, John, ed. *Work: An Inquiry into Christian Thought and Practice.* Baltimore: Helicon Press, 1960.

Toynbee, Arnold J. "Man at Work in the Light of History." In *Man at Work in God's World,* edited by G. E. DeMille. New York: Longmans, Green, 1956.

Underhill, Ruth Murray. *Work-a-day Life of the Pueblos.* Phoenix: Phoenix Indian School, 1946.

Usy, S. H., Jr. *Organization of Work: A Comparative Analysis of Production Among Non-Industrial People.* New Haven: H.R.A.F. Press, 1959.

Van Kaam, Adrian. "The Nurse in the Patient's World." *The American Journal of Nursing* 59 (1959):1680-1710.

Van Kaam, Adrian; Van Croonenburg, Bert; and Muto, Susan. *The Participant Self.* Denville, N.J.: Dimension, 1969.

Weber, Max. *The Protestant Ethic and the Spirit of Capitalism.* Translated by T. Parsons. London: Butler and Tanner, 1948.

Weil, Simone. *La Condition Ouvrière.* Paris: Gallimard, 1951.

Wilensky, H. I. "Varieties of Work Experience." *Man in a World at Work.* Boston: Houghton Mifflin, 1964.

Wyszynski, Stefan Cardinal. *Work.* Translated by Ardle McArdle. Chicago: Scepter Press, 1960.

Yde, J. "Agriculture and Division of Work Among the Waiwai." *Folk* 2 (1960):83-97.

Yolles, S. A. "Mental Health at Work." *To Work Is Human: Mental Health and the Business Community.* New York: Macmillan, 1967.

Zdravomyslov, V.P., and others. *Man and His Work.* Translated and edited by Stephen P. Dunn. White Plains: International Arts and Sciences Press, 1970.

Zerig, Ferdynand. *The Worker in an Affluent Society: Family Life and Industry.* New York: Free Press, 1961.

Zimpel, Lloyd, ed. *Man Against Work.* Grand Rapids: Eerdmans, 1974.